W9-AYH-711

Sacred Celebrations
A Jewish Holiday Handbook

Sacred Celebrations
A Jewish Holiday Handbook

by

Rabbi Ronald H. Isaacs
and
Rabbi Kerry M. Olitzky

KTAV Publishing House, Inc.
Hoboken, New Jersey

Library of Congress Cataloging-in-Publication Data

Isaacs, Ronald H.
    Sacred celebrations : a Jewish holiday handbook / by Ron Isaacs
and Kerry Olitzky.
        p.   cm.
    Includes bibliographical references.
    ISBN 0-88125-484-3 : $19.95. -- ISBN 0-88125-496-7 (pbk.) : $12.95
    1. Fasts and feasts--Judaism. I. Olitzky, Kerry M. II. Title.
BM690.I78   1994
296.4'3--dc20   94-1391
                                                                          CIP

Manufactured in the United States of America

Contents

Preface

The Jewish holidays were formulated to be celebrated and enjoyed, to bring us closer to family and closer to God. Yet for many people, especially those not raised in observant families, the thought of fully celebrating the holidays is a bewildering challenge. Often their children have learned about the holidays at religious school and are eager to celebrate them at home, but the parents are not well versed in basic Judaism and have nowhere to turn for basic information and assistance.

Over the past several years, more and more American Jews have felt the desire to guide their own Jewish learning and religious observances, especially within the context of family. The family approach allows for cooperative learning and celebration. Moreover, it does not limit holiday rituals solely to what will support the interest of the child to the exclusion of the adult, or vice versa. Such a posture, which reflects a Jewish spiritual renewal, also brings the Jewish calendar out of the classroom and into the lives of our people. We believe that this trend toward empowerment is of great importance, and are working to help develop a literature that will support such endeavors of religious growth. *Sacred Celebrations* is a contribution to this enterprise.

It is our contention that Judaism really reflects a bridge between the home and the synagogue. Thus, home and synagogue are both essential to the Jewish family's holiday observances and are both represented in the pages of this book.

Our goal is to be basic but comprehensive, providing all you need to know regarding the holidays and festivals that make up the Jewish religious year (together with some directions for further learning). The Jewish calendar and holiday cycle have a rhythm of their own, and we want to help you to capture it.

Thus, we have prepared this volume as a guide to the family celebration of the Jewish holidays and festivals. It places in one easy-to-use format all of the information you need to guide your family in its celebrations. But this book is more than just a "how-to." It also tells the primary story of each holiday and provides a cultural context for the holiday. While Jewish culture provides the backdrop for most of the information in this book, our holidays also reflect the struggle of our people in its attempt to create a sacred life and a holy world. By celebrating with us, you are helping in the struggle.

Rabbi Ron Isaacs
Rabbi Kerry Olitzky
Tu Bishevat 5754

How to Use This Book

Holidays were fashioned to be celebrated, and this book was created to be used. It was designed to provide you with a basic understanding of the major Jewish holidays and festival celebrations. In order to provide easy access to a wealth of information in a ready-to-use format, the material in each chapter is divided into the following sections:

WORDS OF TORAH
An introduction to the holiday by means of an explanation of a key theme statement from Jewish tradition.

BACK TO BASICS
The basis for the holiday and its celebration.

CALENDAR
The holiday in the context of the Jewish calendar, providing historical background as well. This section helps to establish a relationship to other holidays and an understanding of why we should celebrate it at all.

CELEBRATIONS

In the Synagogue
Includes those aspects of the synagogue service for the holiday that differentiate it from other occasions, such as its Torah or Haftarah reading.

In the Home
The special rituals that take place as part of the home celebration for the holiday.

MAKING FAMILY
Family activities for the holiday, including fun, games, and food.

BASIC BLESSINGS
Major blessings associated with the holiday.

GLOSSARY
Key words and phrases, a basic vocabulary as part of the "culture code" for the holiday.

The Jewish Calendar

The Jewish Calendar

WORDS OF TORAH

Since biblical times, the months and years of the Jewish calendar have been established by the cycles of the moon and the sun. The months are determined by the moon's circuit around the earth. At the same time they must always correspond to the seasons of the year, which are governed by the earth's revolution around the sun.

The Jewish people's attainment of freedom became the beginning point for Israel's historical counting. The Bible, in its account of the liberation from Egypt, says, "This month shall be the beginning of the months, the very first of the month" (Exodus 12:2). The spring season was the beginning of the year according to the Torah, designating both nature's rebirth and the birth of human freedom.

BACK TO BASICS

The ancient Israelites had no calendar. They did know, however, the cycle of the seasons, of planting and harvesting times. Around the year 350 C.E., Hillel II helped to establish a permanent calendar for the Jewish people that coordinated the lunar and solar years with each other. We have followed this calendar ever since.

The Jewish calendar's months are fixed by the cycle of the moon, while the years are fixed by the earth's cycle around the sun. This coordination of lunar and solar phenomena ensures that the Jewish holidays will occur in their proper seasons as specified in the Bible (e.g., Pesach in the spring), even though their dates in the secular civil calendar, which is based only on the earth's movement around the sun, differ each year.

The Hebrew calendar begins in the spring with the month of Nisan, when the Israelites gained freedom from the Egyptians. Our ancestors' return from exile after the First Temple was destroyed occurred in the fall. Our religious New Year, Rosh Hashanah, is celebrated in the fall in the month of Tishri.

CALENDAR

There are twelve lunar months in the Jewish calendar. Each of them has either 29 or 30 days. Since the lunar year thus totals 354 days, while the solar year amounts to 365¼ days, it is necessary to periodically add an extra month in order to reconcile them. Approximately once every three years, a thirteenth month called Adar II is added. A year in which Adar II is intercalated is known as a leap year.

These are the names of the months of the Jewish calendar: (1) Nisan, (2), Iyar, (3) Sivan, (4) Tammuz, (5) Av, (6) Elul, (7) Tishri, (8) Heshvan, (9) Kislev, (10) Tevet, (11) Shevat, (12) Adar, (13) Adar II (only in a leap year).

The Jewish calendar numbers the years from the date of the creation of the world, as determined by Jewish tradition. Thus 5754 (1993–1994) represents the 5,754th year since the beginning of the world, or symbolically, since the beginning of consciously recorded time.

Hillel's calendar firmed the dates of the Jewish festivals. With the exception of the month called Heshvan, every single one of the twelve lunar months has some sort of special day or observance. Here is a brief summary of the dates (or the beginnings) of the Jewish festivals.

14 Nisan	Pesach
27 Nisan	Holocaust Remembrance Day
4 Iyar	Yom Hazikaron
5 Iyar	Yom Ha'atzma'ut
28 Iyar	Yom Yerushalayim
6 Sivan	Shavuot
9 Av	Tisha B'av
1 Tishri	Rosh Hashanah
10 Tishri	Yom Kippur
14 Tishri	Sukkot
22 Tishri	Shemini Atzeret
23 Tishri	Simchat Torah
25 Kislev	Hanukkah
15 Shevat	Tu Bishevat
14 Adar	Purim

CELEBRATIONS

In the Synagogue

There are several synagogue celebrations directly related to the association of the moon's renewal. The first is Rosh Hodesh, the beginning of every Jewish month, which is celebrated as a minor holy day for one day. The date of Rosh Hodesh is always announced in the Sabbath synagogue service of the preceding week. Rosh Hodesh is celebrated in the synagogue by the recitation of a shortened version of the Hallel psalms of praise. An extra Torah portion (Numbers 28:1–16) is read which describes the ancient sacrifices which our biblical ancestors offered on Rosh Hodesh. The Musaf additional service includes a plea for a month of blessing and prosperity.

Although there are no work restrictions on Rosh Hodesh, Jewish tradition has used it as an occasion to honor women for their unusual piety by allowing them a reprieve from their usual work.

The second celebration of the moon's renewal is called Kiddush L'vanah, the sanctification of the moon. Several days after the emergence of the new moon, those who observe this ritual assemble in the open to offer a prayer of thanksgiving for the renewal of life and hope for the future. The worshippers then bid farewell to each other with the words *Shalom aleikhem* ("Peace be with you") and *Aleikhem shalom* ("And with you, peace").

The last celebration takes place only once every twenty-eight years. It is called the Birkat Hachamah, the blessing of the sun. When the cycle of the heavenly bodies completes itself at the spring equinox every twenty-eight years, we give thanks to God for the sun. The last time this blessing was said was April 9, 1991.

BASIC BLESSINGS

Kiddush L'vanah

בָּרוּךְ אַתָּה יְיָ אֱלֹהֵנוּ מֶלֶךְ הָעוֹלָם אֲשֶׁר בְּמַאֲמָרוֹ בָּרָא שְׁחָקִים
וּבְרוּחַ פִּיו־כָּל צְבָאָם חֹק וּזְמַן נָתַן לָהֶם שֶׁלֹּא יְשַׁנּוּ אֶת תַּפְקִידָם
שָׂשִׂים וּשְׂמֵחִים לַעֲשׂוֹת רְצוֹן קוֹנָם פּוֹעֵל אֱמֶת שֶׁפְּעֻלָּתוֹ אֱמֶת
וְלַלְּבָנָה אָמַר שֶׁתִּתְחַדֵּשׁ עֲטֶרֶת תִּפְאֶרֶת לַעֲמוּסֵי בָטֶן שֶׁהֵם
עֲתִידִים לְהִתְחַדֵּשׁ כְּמוֹתָהּ וּלְפָאֵר לְיוֹצְרָם עַל שֵׁם כְּבוֹד מַלְכוּתוֹ
בָּרוּךְ אַתָּה יְיָ מְחַדֵּשׁ חֳדָשִׁים

Barukh atah adonai eloheinu melekh ha'olam asher b'ma'amaro bara sh'chakim uv'ru'ach piv kol tz'va'am chok uz'man natan lahem shelo y'shanu et tafkidam sassim us'meichim la'asot r'tzon konam po'eil emet shep'ulato emet v'lal'vana amar shetitchadeish ateret tiferet la'amusei vaten sheheim atidim l'hitchadeish k'mota ul'fa'eir l'yotzram al sheim k'vod malkhuto. Barukh atah adonai m'chadeish chadashim.

Praised are You, Adonai our God, Sovereign of the Universe, whose word created the heavens, whose breath created all that they contain. God gave them laws and seasons so that they would not deviate from their assigned tasks. Gladly they do the will of their Creator. God spoke to the moon: renew yourself, crown of glory for those who were borne in the womb, who are also destined to be renewed. Praised are You, God, who renews the months.

Birkat Hachamah

בָּרוּךְ אַתָּה יְיָ אֱלֹהֵנוּ מֶלֶךְ הָעוֹלָם עוֹשֶׂה מַעֲשֶׂה בְרֵאשִׁית

Barukh atah adonai eloheinu melekh ha'olam oseh ma'aseh v'reishit.

Praised are You, Adonai our God, Sovereign of the Universe, who makes the work of creation.

MAKING FAMILY

1. Play the Moon Game with your family. Here is a description of the game.

Purpose
To review the Hebrew dates of the holidays and to identify the appearance of the moon on a given holiday.

Materials
Six drawings representing the six phases of the moon.

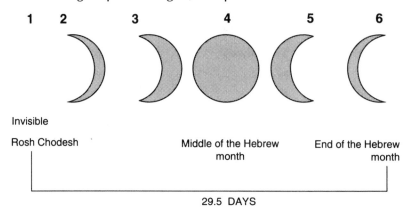

Instructions

a. Rest the drawings of the moon phases on a ledge or attach to a felt board.
b. Have the family leader name a Jewish holiday and its date and ask the participants to pick the correct drawing of the moon. For example,

Rosh Hashanah 1 Tishri   invisible
Pesach   15 Nisan   full moon
Hanukkah   25 Kislev   [ins. picture]

GLOSSARY

Adar II. Extra month added during leap year in the Jewish calendar.
Birkat Hachamah. Blessing of the sun, occurring once every twenty-eight years.
Kiddush L'vanah. Blessing of the New Moon.
Lu'ach. Calendar.
Rosh Hodesh. The first day of each Jewish month.

Celebrating a Jewish Home

Celebrating a Jewish Home

WORDS OF TORAH

Our homes are small sanctuaries, our tables reminiscent of the altar in the ancient Temple in Jerusalem. Thus, we strive to bring sparks of the holy into our homes, ever-mindful of God's presence in our lives. According to Deuteronomy 6:9 and 11:20, we are instructed to "write them [the words of Torah] on the *mezuzot* of our homes and gates." This serves as a physical reminder of the covenant established at Sinai between God and the Jewish people; we try to live lives and nurture families reflective of that covenant.

BACK TO BASICS

Lots of things turn a house into a home. One thing is designating the fact that a Jewish family lives here through the placement of a mezuzah. While the term *mezuzah* technically refers to the doorpost, it has come to mean the holder for the parchment which is then affixed to the doorpost.

The parchment in the mezuzah is made from the skin of a kosher animal. On it is written the Shema Yisrael and Deuteronomy 6:4–9, 11:13–31.

Mezuzah parchments should be checked twice every seven years. Remember that according to Jewish tradition, only a handwritten parchment should be inserted in the mezuzah and not a slip of paper bearing a printed text.

CALENDAR

Since one is required to affix the mezuzah no more than thirty days after moving into a new home, it is often associated with the housewarming, which in Hebrew is called *chanukat habayit*, the dedication of a new home.

CELEBRATIONS

In the Synagogue

While mezuzot historically were not affixed to public institutions like synagogues (unless there were Jews residing there), other traditions have developed which help to direct the thoughts of worshippers. The *shivviti* plaque (from the verse in Psalms 16:8, "I have set Adonai before me," part of the daily liturgy) served as a focal point for Jewish prayer and was placed in front of those praying. Eventually, this and other verses (such as "Know before Whom you stand") were inscribed above the Aron Kodesh (holy ark) which houses the Sifrei Torah (Torah scrolls).

In the Home

The parchment in the mezuzah is to be rolled up so that the word Shaddai, one of the names of God, is on the outside. The mezuzah should be affixed on the upper third of the right-hand door frame as you enter the house (and on the doors of other rooms too), but no less than the width of your hand from the top of the door frame. The top of the mezuzah should be on a diagonal, leaning toward the house.

In addition to the mezuzah, one needs to be reminded of the direction of Jerusalem, since you are supposed to face toward Jerusalem while praying. The eastern wall of one's home is marked with a mizrach plaque, the name of which is taken from the verse: "From the rising [*mi-mizrach*] of the sun until it goes down, Adonai is to be praised" (Psalms 113:3). The mizrach plaque is important but not essential, for the rabbis tell us, "If you can't figure it out, then direct your heart toward Jerusalem" (Babylonian Talmud, Baba Batra 25a).

BASIC BLESSINGS

On Affixing the Mezuzah

בָּרוּךְ אַתָּה יהוה אֱלֹהֵינוּ מֶלֶךְ הָעוֹלָם, אֲשֶׁר קִדְּשָׁנוּ בְּמִצְוֹתָיו וְצִוָּנוּ לִקְבּוֹעַ מְזוּזָה.

Barukh atah adonai eloheinu melekh ha'olam asher kid'shanu b'mitzvotav v'tzivanu likbo'a m'zuzah.

Praised are You, Adonai our God, Sovereign of the Universe, who has made us holy by mitzvot and instructed us to affix the mezuzah.

בָּרוּךְ אַתָּה יהוה אֱלֹהֵינוּ מֶלֶךְ הָעוֹלָם, שֶׁהֶחֱיָנוּ וְקִיְּמָנוּ וְהִגִּיעָנוּ לַזְּמַן הַזֶּה.

Barukh atah adonai eloheinu melekh ha'olam shehecheyanu v'kimanu v'higi'anu laz'man hazeh.

Praised are You, Adonai our God, Sovereign of the Universe, who has kept us alive, sustained us, and helped us to reach this moment.

MAKING FAMILY

1. Whenever you affix a mezuzah, whether you have just moved into your house or apartment or not, celebrate the dedication of your home (and of your family to Torah).
2. While the parchment must be prepared according to specific regulations, the mezuzah does not have to be. Therefore, together prepare a case for the parchment that represents your family.
3. Some people like to put the mezuzah on the door to a child's room somewhat lower than normal so that the child can see and touch it on entering the room.
4. Get into the habit of kissing the mezuzah as you enter, especially the first time you enter a new house or room.

GLOSSARY

Klaf. The parchment inside the mezuzah.

Kuzo b'mukhsaz kuzo. Phrase on the back of the mezuzah parchment which stands for Adonai Eloheinu Adonai.

Mezuzah. Technically the doorpost, but people use the term to refer to the case and the parchment.

Mizrach. Literally, "east," referring to the plaque which designates the eastern wall in the house, so that one knows which way to face during prayer.

Shaddai. "Almighty God," one of God's names and also an acronym for *Shomeir D'latot yisra'eil*, meaning "Protector of Israel."

Rosh Hodesh

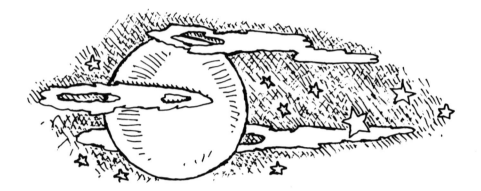

Rosh Hodesh

WORDS OF TORAH

In biblical times, Rosh Hodesh, the day on which a new Jewish month begins, was a minor festival in the life of the Israelite people. On this day, special sacrificial offerings were made in honor of the proclamation of the new month. In addition, the shofar (ram's horn) was sounded, as it is written in Psalms 81:4, chosen as the psalm recited every Thursday morning: "Sound the shofar on the new moon, on the full moon for the festive day."

Today for many Jewish people Rosh Hodesh serves as a time of reflection and renewal. It provides an opportunity to look at the month past and suggest ways of improving on it in the new month ahead.

BACK TO BASICS

Rosh Hodesh is mentioned both in the Bible and in rabbinic writings as a day of special importance. Although there are no work restrictions today on Rosh Hodesh, the Jerusalem Talmud records that in ancient Israel women abstained from work. Traditional women today usually do not work on Rosh Hodesh. This special dispensation was awarded to them by the rabbis because the women of Israel refused to donate their jewelry toward the making of the golden calf.

In ancient times, when the day of Rosh Hodesh was determined not by consulting a calendar but by the rabbinical court, based on reports by witnesses who had observed the new moon, people would assemble for a festive meal and special prayers would be read. Today, by astronomical calculation, the beginning of the new month takes place at the moment when the moon is exactly between the earth and the sun, and thus nothing is visible of the moon. It is then that the *molad,* or birth of the moon, takes place.

CALENDAR

Long ago, the beginning of a new month was declared when two independent witnesses reported to the Sanhedrin (rabbinical court) that the crescent of a new moon had appeared. The declaration was relayed from city to city by lighting signal fires on the hilltops. Sometimes false fires were lit by non-Jews who wanted to confuse and delay the announcement of the new month. To make certain that all the holidays were still celebrated on their proper day even if this happened, an extra day was added to Rosh Hodesh. As a result, Rosh Hodesh continues to be observed for two days by most Jewish communities all over the world, with the exception of Israel. The Reform movement has generally chosen to defer to the scientific exactitude of modern calendation.

It takes about 29½ days for the moon to make a circuit around the earth. Since half-days are not possible, some Jewish months are 29 days whereas others are 30. If a month contains 30 days, then the last day of that month and the first day of the next month comprise Rosh Hodesh. If a month contains only 29 days, then only the first day of the following month is Rosh Hodesh.

CELEBRATIONS

In the Synagogue

A special prayer announcing the new month is recited in the synagogue on the Sabbath preceding Rosh Hodesh (with the exception of the month of Tishri). This prayer asks for God's blessings of prosperity and good health.

The worship service on Rosh Hodesh includes the Torah reading which describes the special sacrificial offerings for Rosh Hodesh (Numbers 28:1–15). The service also includes selections from the Hallel psalms of praise and a special additional Musaf service. Some congregations sound the shofar on Rosh Hodesh (except if it falls on the Sabbath), following the ancient biblical custom.

In the Home

There is no lighting of festival candles in the home on Rosh Hodesh, since it is a minor festival. Some traditional women try to abstain from work on Rosh Hodesh. They often have special get-togethers which include both study and socializing among themselves. Other families try to serve a new food on Rosh Hodesh as a sign of renewal.

MAKING FAMILY

1. Go outside and announce as a family the arrival of the new moon. After seeing it, sing *Siman tov u'mazal tov.*
2. Discuss as a family your hopes and wishes for the new month.
3. Make cookies in the shapes of the moon's various phases (crescent, half-moon, etc.) and serve them on Rosh Hodesh.

4. Create decorations in the form of streamers and write appropriate biblical verses on them. Add glitter-in-the dark stars to them and hang them in various rooms in your home to create the illusion of a night sky.
5. Have the men in your home do some special chores that the women would normally do, as a remembrance of the special dispensation for women on Rosh Hodesh.

GLOSSARY

L'vanah. "Moon."

Molad. The "birth" of the moon (i.e., its first appearance in the sky).

Shabbat M'var'khim. The Sabbath on which the prayer for the new moon is recited.

Shabbat

Shabbat

WORDS OF TORAH

The origin of Shabbat goes back to the beginning of creation. The Bible relates that God made the world in six days and rested on the seventh, thereby blessing it. Since that time the Sabbath has remained the holiest day of the year for Jewish people, despite its occurring fifty-two successive times. It is not only a sacred day but one that is filled with joy and delight. It's a time to pray, relax, and rejuvenate ourselves. It is a time to be together as a family. Ahad Ha'Am, a famous Jewish philosopher, once said, "More than Israel has kept the Sabbath, the Sabbath has kept Israel."

BACK TO BASICS

The Sabbath is the only holiday included in the Ten Commandments. The fourth commandment says, "Six days you shall labor and do all of your work, but the seventh day is a sabbath of God: you shall not do any work" (Exodus 20:9-10). Observing Shabbat gives people an opportunity to rest their minds and bodies, as well as an opportunity to express their appreciation for many of the things that they are often too busy to notice during the week. It is a time to be with friends and family, and an occasion to reflect on the past week before beginning the new one. Abraham Joshua Heschel, the noted Jewish theologian, once said, "The most important ingredient in creating a Jewish home is the celebration of the Shabbat."

CALENDAR

Of all of the festivals of the Jewish year, Shabbat is the only weekly one. Although it officially begins with sundown on Friday, it really begins earlier. Preparing for it ahead of time is also part of the holiday, and the work begins to intensify as the week draws to a close. Since Shabbat has been portrayed in Jewish mystical tradition as a bride or a queen who visits our homes every week of the year, we are expected to ready ourselves physically and spiritually to greet our honored guest. The house is cleaned, the candlesticks and Kiddush cup for wine are polished. We too wash ourselves and put on fresh clothing. The Shabbat table is set with our best dinnerware, a pretty tablecloth, sacramental wine, flowers, and two challot. It is great fun to include the entire family in these preparations and to do things to foster anticipation of this much-awaited day. To add to the mood of caring and sharing, many families drop some coins in a tzedakah (charity) box just before the lighting of the Shabbat candles.

CELEBRATIONS

In the Synagogue
Shabbat is primarily a home-oriented occasion, although there are several synagogue prayer services that take place both Friday evening and Saturday morning, afternoon and evening. Praying on Shabbat in synagogue serves to lift our spirit above mundane concerns.

Welcoming the Sabbath Bride has become part of the Shabbat Friday evening service, which is called Kabbalat Shabbat ("Welcoming the Sabbath"). Some communities have early Friday services at sundown, allowing families to attend them and return home to a leisurely Shabbat meal. Other communities have late Friday evening services which are attended following the family Shabbat meal.

During the Friday night service, the well-known tune Lecha Dodi ("Come, my beloved") is sung. Following is the evening service, including the chanting of the Shabbat Kiddush over a cup of wine. The Shabbat morning and afternoon services include the reading of the Torah. (Some Reform congregations read the Torah on Friday evening as well.) Each week a different portion of the Torah is read, highlighting yet another series of adventures in the life of the Jewish people. Many rabbis use the Torah portion as the basis for a sermon (called a *d'var torah*) or for a discussion with the congregation. The Shabbat service is a wonderful time for Bar and Bat Mitzvah ceremonies. Babies are often given their Hebrew names during the Shabbat morning service, and brides and grooms are often called to the Torah on that morning for special honors. The evening service that night concludes with a beautiful ceremony known as Havdalah ("separation") which helps bid farewell to the holy Shabbat.

Many communities now have special Shabbat services for young people, geared to their abilities, interests, and attention span. These often include the use of puppets, stories, games, and Shabbat songs.

In the Home

The act of lighting Shabbat candles before sunset marks the actual beginning of the Sabbath. A famous Jewish legend tells us that Adam opened his eyes on the eve of Shabbat and found himself in the dark shadows of the Garden of Eden. He was very afraid when suddenly he stumbled upon two stones. He picked them up and struck them, starting a fire. Feeling the warmth as a gift from God, it was then that Adam spoke the very first blessing ever heard on earth:

"Praised are You, God, Sovereign of the Universe, who creates the light of the fire."

Although it is customary for women to light the Shabbat candles, Jewish tradition permits (and we encourage) men to also perform the ritual. It is customary for parents to bless their children before sitting down to the Sabbath meal. This provides them with a wonderful opportunity to express appreciation for their children. Through the touch of a parent's hands or the sound of a parent's voice, children can feel and respond to the love their family has for them. Let your children bless you as well—and one another.

Because happiness and joy are synonymous with Shabbat, it has become customary to begin the meal by reciting the blessing over a cup of wine, called the Kiddush. The Kiddush says thank you to God for creating the world and giving us Shabbat. Washing of the hands (*n'tilat yadayim* in Hebrew) with a blessing follows the Kiddush. It is the Jewish way of sanctifying the act of eating. This is followed by the blessing over bread, called Hamotzi. The bread eaten on Shabbat (and festivals too) is usually a braided loaf called challah. It is traditional to place two challot on the table, recalling the double portion of manna God provided for the Israelites in the desert on the eve of the Sabbath.

Following all of these blessings is the Shabbat meal, which provides the family with an opportunity to enjoy one another's company while eating at a more leisurely pace. The festive food and singing of *z'mirot* (Sabbath songs) between courses adds to the delight of the meal.

Reciting the blessing after the meal (Birkat Hamazon) serves as our expression of appreciation for God's generosity in satisfying us with such a festive meal.

The sequence of rituals performed at the midday Shabbat meal, eaten after the family returns home from synagogue services, follows that of the Friday evening celebration, with some variations.

Shabbat afternoon is a time for a variety of experiences that change the constant pace of daily life. Some people take a nap to refresh their energies. Others use the time for reading or study, alone or with friends. A traditional text for study on Shabbat afternoon is *Pirkei Avot*, known in English as the *Ethics of the Fathers*. For children, special Shabbat games and stories can fill the leisurely afternoon with many pleasurable activities.

The last Shabbat meal on Saturday is called the *se'udah sh'lishit* ("third meal"). It is usually a simple dairy meal. For even this simplest meal, it is still customary to perform the blessings over the hands and bread, sing Shabbat songs, and chant the blessing after the meal.

The ritual conclusion of Shabbat is deferred until about an hour after sunset. When three stars are visible in the sky, it is time for the Havdalah ("separation") service. As a home ceremony, Havdalah is especially appealing because it makes use of all of our senses. The Havdalah ceremony uses a wine cup and a plate, a spice box containing aromatic spices (cloves or cinnamon), and a special braided candle that has more than one wick. The blessing over the wine sanctifies our reentry into the secular world. The blessing over the spices symbolically ensures that the memory of Shabbat will be sweet and lingering. And the blessing over the braided kindle reminds us of God's first creation of light.

When the Havdalah ceremony concludes, everyone present wishes the other a *shavu'a tov* ("good week").

BASIC BLESSINGS

Candlelighting

בָּרוּךְ אַתָּה יהוה אֱלֹהֵינוּ מֶלֶךְ הָעוֹלָם, אֲשֶׁר קִדְּשָׁנוּ בְּמִצְוֹתָיו וְצִוָּנוּ לְהַדְלִיק נֵר שֶׁל שַׁבָּת.

Barukh atah adonai eloheinu melekh ha'olam asher kid'shanu b'mitzvotav v'tzivanu l'hadlik neir shel shabbat.

Praised are You, Adonai our God, Sovereign of the universe, who has made us holy by mitzvot and instructed us to light the Shabbat candles.

Family Blessings

For boys. Parents approach each son, place their hands on his head, and recite:

יְשִׂימְךָ אֱלֹהִים כְּאֶפְרַיִם וְכִמְנַשֶּׁה.

Y'simkha elohim k'ephrayim vekhim'nasheh.

May God make you as Ephraim and Manasseh (Genesis 48:20).

For girls. Parents approach each daughter, place both their hands upon her head, and recite:

יְשִׂימֵךְ אֱלֹהִים כְּשָׂרָה, רִבְקָה, רָחֵל, וְלֵאָה.

Y'simeikh elohim k'sarah rivkah rachel v'leah.

May God make you as Sarah, Rebekkah, Rachel, and Leah.

For both boys and girls. Conclude with the priestly blessing:

יְבָרֶכְךָ יְיָ וְיִשְׁמְרֶךָ.
יָאֵר יְיָ פָּנָיו אֵלֶיךָ וִיחֻנֶּךָּ.
יִשָּׂא יְיָ פָּנָיו אֵלֶיךָ וְיָשֵׂם לְךָ שָׁלוֹם.

Y'varekh'kha adonai v'yishm'rekha
Ya'er adonai panav e'lekha vichuneka
Yisa adonai panav e'lekha v'yasem l'kha shalom.

May God bless you and keep you.
May God deal kindly and graciously with you.
May God bestow favor on you and give you (the gift of knowing) peace.

Kiddush (Blessing Over the Wine)

וַיְהִי עֶרֶב וַיְהִי בֹקֶר יוֹם הַשִּׁשִּׁי. וַיְכֻלּוּ הַשָּׁמַיִם וְהָאָרֶץ וְכָל־צְבָאָם: וַיְכַל אֱלֹהִים בַּיּוֹם הַשְּׁבִיעִי, מְלַאכְתּוֹ אֲשֶׁר עָשָׂה, וַיִּשְׁבֹּת בַּיּוֹם הַשְּׁבִיעִי, מִכָּל־מְלַאכְתּוֹ אֲשֶׁר עָשָׂה: וַיְבָרֶךְ אֱלֹהִים אֶת־יוֹם הַשְּׁבִיעִי, וַיְקַדֵּשׁ אֹתוֹ, כִּי בוֹ שָׁבַת מִכָּל־מְלַאכְתּוֹ, אֲשֶׁר־בָּרָא אֱלֹהִים לַעֲשׂוֹת:

בָּרוּךְ אַתָּה יהוה אֱלֹהֵינוּ מֶלֶךְ הָעוֹלָם, בּוֹרֵא פְּרִי הַגָּפֶן. בָּרוּךְ אַתָּה יהוה אֱלֹהֵינוּ מֶלֶךְ הָעוֹלָם, אֲשֶׁר קִדְּשָׁנוּ בְּמִצְוֹתָיו וְרָצָה בָנוּ, וְשַׁבָּת קָדְשׁוֹ בְּאַהֲבָה וּבְרָצוֹן הִנְחִילָנוּ, זִכָּרוֹן לְמַעֲשֵׂה בְרֵאשִׁית. כִּי הוּא יוֹם תְּחִלָּה לְמִקְרָאֵי קֹדֶשׁ, זֵכֶר לִיצִיאַת מִצְרָיִם. כִּי בָנוּ בָחַרְתָּ וְאוֹתָנוּ קִדַּשְׁתָּ מִכָּל־הָעַמִּים, וְשַׁבָּת קָדְשְׁךָ בְּאַהֲבָה וּבְרָצוֹן הִנְחַלְתָּנוּ. בָּרוּךְ אַתָּה יְיָ, מְקַדֵּשׁ הַשַּׁבָּת.

Vay'hi erev vay'hi voker yom hashishi. Vay'khulu hashamayim v'ha'aretz v'khol tz'va'am. Vay'khal elohim bayom hash'vi'i m'lachto asher asah vayishbot bayom

*hash'vi'i mikol m'lakhto asher asah. Vay'varekh elohim et
yom hash'vi'i vay'kadeish oto ki vo shavat mikol m'lakhto
asher bara elohim la'asot.*

*Barukh atah adonai eloheinu melekh ha'olam borei p'ri
hagafen*
*Barukh atah adonai eloheinu melekh ha'olam asher
kid'shanu b'mitzvotav v'ratza vanu v'shabbat kodsho
b'ahavah uv'ratzon hinchilanu zikaron l'ma'aseh v'reishit.
Ki hu yom t'chilah l'mikra'ei kodesh zecher litzi'at
mitzrayim. Ki vanu vacharta v'otanu kidashta mikol
ha'amim v'shabbat kodshekha b'ahavah uv'ratzon
hinchaltanu. Barukh atah adonai m'kadeish hashabbat.*

There was evening and there was morning, the sixth day.
The heavens and the earth, and all they contain, were
completed. On the seventh day God finished the work.
God ceased on the seventh day from all work and blessed
the seventh day and called it holy, because on it God
ceased from all the work of creation.

Praised are You, Adonai, Sovereign of the Universe, who
creates the fruit of the vine.
Praised are You, Adonai, Sovereign of the Universe, who
has made us holy by mitzvot and has been pleased with
us. You have lovingly and gladly granted us Your holy
Sabbath, recalling the creation of the world. The Sabbath
is first among the days of sacred assembly, sanctifying us
among all people by granting us Your holy Sabbath lovingly
and gladly. Praised are You, God, who sanctifies the
Sabbath.

N'tilat Yadayim (Washing the Hands)

Grasp a cup or pitcher of water in your left hand and pour some over the right. Reverse the process and repeat once or twice. Recite this blessing:

בָּרוּךְ אַתָּה יהוה אֱלֹהֵינוּ מֶלֶךְ הָעוֹלָם, אֲשֶׁר קִדְּשָׁנוּ בְּמִצְוֹתָיו וְצִוָּנוּ עַל נְטִילַת יָדַיִם.

Barukh atah adonai eloheinu melekh ha'olam asher kid'shanu b'mitzvotav v'tzivanu al n'tilat yadayim.

Praised are You, Adonai, Sovereign of the Universe, who has made us holy by mitzvot and instructed us to wash our hands.

Hamotzi (Blessing Over the Bread)

Remove the covering over the two challot and recite this blessing:

בָּרוּךְ אַתָּה יהוה אֱלֹהֵינוּ מֶלֶךְ הָעוֹלָם, הַמּוֹצִיא לֶחֶם מִן הָאָרֶץ.

Barukh atah adonai eloheinu melekh ha'olam hamotzi lechem min ha'aretz.

Praised are You, Adonai our God, Sovereign of the Universe, who brings forth bread from the earth.

Birkat Hamazon (Blessing after the Meal)

רַבּוֹתַי נְבָרֵךְ.

Rabotai n'vareikh

Friends, let us give thanks.

The others respond, and the leader repeats:

יְהִי שֵׁם יְיָ מְבֹרָךְ מֵעַתָּה וְעַד עוֹלָם.

Y'hi sheim adonai m'vorakh mei'atah v'ad olam.

May God be praised now and forever.

The leader continues:

בִּרְשׁוּת רַבּוֹתַי, נְבָרֵךְ (אֱלֹהֵינוּ) שֶׁאָכַלְנוּ מִשֶּׁלוֹ.

Bir'shut rabotai n'vareikh (eloheinu) she'akhalnu mishelo.

With your consent friends, let us praise (our God) the One of whose food we have partaken.

The others respond, and the leader repeats:

בָּרוּךְ (אֱלֹהֵינוּ) שֶׁאָכַלְנוּ מִשֶּׁלוֹ וּבְטוּבוֹ חָיִינוּ.

Barukh (eloheinu) she'akhalnu mishelo uv'tuvo chayinu.

Praised be (our God) the One whose food we have partaken and by whose goodness we live.

Leader and others:

בָּרוּךְ הוּא וּבָרוּךְ שְׁמוֹ.

Barukh hu uvarukh sh'mo.

Praised be God and praised be God's name.

בָּרוּךְ אַתָּה יהוה אֱלֹהֵינוּ מֶלֶךְ הָעוֹלָם, הַזָּן אֶת הָעוֹלָם כֻּלּוֹ בְּטוּבוֹ, בְּחֵן בְּחֶסֶד וּבְרַחֲמִים. הוּא נוֹתֵן לֶחֶם לְכָל בָּשָׂר כִּי

לְעוֹלָם חַסְדּוֹ. וּבְטוּבוֹ הַגָּדוֹל תָּמִיד לֹא חָסַר לָנוּ וְאַל יֶחְסַר לָנוּ
מָזוֹן לְעוֹלָם וָעֶד בַּעֲבוּר שְׁמוֹ הַגָּדוֹל, כִּי הוּא אֵל זָן וּמְפַרְנֵס לַכֹּל
וּמֵטִיב לַכֹּל וּמֵכִין מָזוֹן לְכָל־בְּרִיּוֹתָיו אֲשֶׁר בָּרָא. בָּרוּךְ אַתָּה
יהוה, הַזָּן אֶת הַכֹּל.

*Barukh atah adonai, eloheinu melekh ha'olam, hazan et
ha'olam kulo b'tuvo b'chein, b'chesed, uv'rachamim. Hu
notein lechem l'khol basar, ki l'olam chasdo. Uv'tuvo hagadol, tamid lo chasar lanu, v'al yechsar lanu mazon l'olam
va'ed ba'avur sh'mo hagadol, ki hu el zan um'farneis lakol,
umeitiv lakol, umeikhin mazon l'khol b'riyotav asher bara.
Barukh atah adonai, hazan et hakol.*

Praised are You, Eternal, our God, Sovereign of the Universe who sustains the whole world with kindness and
compassion. You provide food for every creature, for
Your love endures forever. Your great goodness has never
failed us. Your great glory assures us nourishment. All life
is God's creation and God is good to all, providing every
creature with food and sustenance. Praised are You, God
who sustains all life.

נוֹדֶה לְךָ יְיָ אֱלֹהֵינוּ עַל שֶׁהִנְחַלְתָּ לַאֲבוֹתֵינוּ אֶרֶץ חֶמְדָּה טוֹבָה
וּרְחָבָה, בְּרִית וְתוֹרָה, חַיִּים וּמָזוֹן. יִתְבָּרַךְ שִׁמְךָ בְּפִי כָל־חַי תָּמִיד
לְעוֹלָם וָעֶד, כַּכָּתוּב: וְאָכַלְתָּ וְשָׂבָעְתָּ וּבֵרַכְתָּ אֶת־יְיָ אֱלֹהֶיךָ עַל
הָאָרֶץ הַטּוֹבָה אֲשֶׁר נָתַן לָךְ. בָּרוּךְ אַתָּה יְיָ, עַל הָאָרֶץ וְעַל
הַמָּזוֹן.

*Nodeh l'kha adonai eloheinu al shehinchalta la'avoteinu
eretz chemdah, tovah ur'chavah, b'rit v'torah, chayim um-
azon. Yitbarakh shimkha b'fi khol chai tamid l'olam va'ed.*

Kakatuv v'akhalta v'savata uvayrakhta et adonai elohekha
al ha'aretz hatovah asher natan lakh. Barukh atah adonai,
al ha'aretz v'al hamazon.

We thank you, God, for the pleasing, ample, desirable
land which You gave to our ancestors, for the covenant
and Torah, for life and sustenance. May You forever be
praised by all who live, as it is written in the Torah:
"When you have eaten and are satisfied, you shall praise
the Eternal your God for the good land which God has
given you." Praised are You, God, for the land and for
sustenance.

וּבְנֵה יְרוּשָׁלַיִם עִיר הַקֹּדֶשׁ בִּמְהֵרָה בְיָמֵינוּ. בָּרוּךְ אַתָּה יְיָ, בּוֹנֶה
בְרַחֲמָיו יְרוּשָׁלָיִם. אָמֵן.

Uv'neih yerushalayim ir hakodesh bimheirah v'yameinu.
Barukh atah adonai, boneh v'rachamav yerushalayim.
Amen.

Fully rebuild Jerusalem, the holy city, soon in our time.
Praised are You, Adonai, who in mercy rebuilds Jerusalem.
Amen.

בָּרוּךְ אַתָּה יהוה אֱלֹהֵינוּ מֶלֶךְ הָעוֹלָם, הַמֶּלֶךְ הַטּוֹב וְהַמֵּטִיב
לַכֹּל. הוּא הֵטִיב, הוּא מֵטִיב, הוּא יֵיטִיב לָנוּ. הוּא גְמָלָנוּ הוּא
גוֹמְלֵנוּ הוּא יִגְמְלֵנוּ לָעַד חֵן וָחֶסֶד וְרַחֲמִים וִיזַכֵּנוּ לִימוֹת הַמָּשִׁיחַ.

Barukh atah adonai, eloheinu melekh ha'olam, hamelekh
hatov v'hameitiv lakol. Hu heitiv, hu meitiv, hu yeitiv
lanu. Hu g'malanu, hu gomleinu, hu yigm'leinu la'ad chein
vachesed v'rachamim, vizakeinu limot hamashi'ach.

Praised are You, God, Sovereign of the Universe who is good to all, whose goodness is constant through all time. Favor us with kindness and compassion now and in the future as in the past. May we be worthy of the days of the Messiah.

הָרַחֲמָן, הוּא יַנְחִילֵנוּ יוֹם שֶׁכֻּלוֹ שַׁבָּת וּמְנוּחָה לְחַיֵּי הָעוֹלָמִים.

Harachaman hu yanchileinu yom shekulo shabbat umenu-chah l'chayei ha'olamim.

May the Merciful grant us a day of true shabbat rest, reflecting the life of eternity.

[On festivals:

הָרַחֲמָן, הוּא יַנְחִילֵנוּ יוֹם שֶׁכֻּלוֹ טוֹב

Harachaman hu yanchileinu yom shekulo tov.

May the Merciful grant us a day filled with the spirit of the festival.]

וְנִשָׂא בְרָכָה מֵאֵת יְיָ וּצְדָקָה מֵאֱלֹהֵי יִשְׁעֵנוּ וְנִמְצָא חֵן וְשֵׂכֶל טוֹב בְּעֵינֵי אֱלֹהִים וְאָדָם. עֹשֶׂה שָׁלוֹם בִּמְרוֹמָיו הוּא יַעֲשֶׂה שָׁלוֹם עָלֵינוּ וְעַל כָּל-יִשְׂרָאֵל, וְאִמְרוּ אָמֵן.
V'nisa v'rakhah mei'eit adonai utz'dakah mei'elohei yish'einu. V'nimtza chein v'seikhel tov b'einei elohim v'adam. Oseh shalom bimromav hu ya'aseh shalom aleinu v'al kol yisra'eil. V'imru amen.

May we receive blessings from God, loving-kindness from the God of our deliverance. May we find grace and good favor before God and all people. May God who brings peace to the universe bring peace to us and to all the people Israel. And let us say: Amen.

Midday Shabbat Blessing over Wine

וְשָׁמְרוּ בְנֵי־יִשְׂרָאֵל אֶת הַשַׁבָּת לַעֲשׂוֹת אֶת־הַשַׁבָּת לְדֹרֹתָם בְּרִית
עוֹלָם: בֵּינִי וּבֵין בְּנֵי יִשְׂרָאֵל אוֹת הִיא לְעֹלָם כִּי שֵׁשֶׁת יָמִים
עָשָׂה יְיָ אֶת־הַשָׁמַיִם וְאֶת־הָאָרֶץ וּבַיּוֹם הַשְׁבִיעִי שָׁבַת וַיִּנָּפַשׁ:

*V'shamru v'nai yisra'eil et hashabbat la'asot et hashabbat
l'dorotam b'rit olam. Beini uvein b'nai yisra'eil ot hi l'olam
ki sheishet yamim asah adonai et hashamayim v'et ha'aretz
uvayom hash'vi'i shavat vayinafash.*

The children of Israel shall keep the Sabbath, observing it
throughout all generations as an everlasting covenant for
all time: it shall be a sign for all time between Me and
the children of Israel. For in six days God made heaven
and earth, and on the seventh day God ceased from
work and was refreshed.

*A modified version of the Kiddush is then recited over a cup
of wine.*

עַל כֵּן בֵּרַךְ יהוה אֶת יוֹם הַשַׁבָּת וַיְקַדְּשֵׁהוּ
בָּרוּךְ אַתָּה יהוה אֱלֹהֵינוּ מֶלֶךְ הָעוֹלָם, בּוֹרֵא פְּרִי הַגָּפֶן.

*Al ken berach adonai et yom hashabbat vay'kad'sheihu.
Barukh atah adonai eloheinu melekh ha'olam borei p'ri
hagafen.*

Therefore God blessed the Sabbath day and made it
holy.
Praised are You, God, Sovereign of the Universe, who
creates the fruit of the vine.

Havdalah

The person who leads the Havdalah ceremony raises the cup of wine and says:

בָּרוּךְ אַתָּה יהוה אֱלֹהֵינוּ מֶלֶךְ הָעוֹלָם, בּוֹרֵא פְּרִי הַגָּפֶן.

Barukh atah adonai eloheinu melekh ha'olam borei p'ri hagafen.

Praised are You, Adonai, Sovereign of the Universe, who creates the fruit of the vine.

Next, he or she lifts the spice box and says:

בָּרוּךְ אַתָּה יהוה אֱלֹהֵינוּ מֶלֶךְ הָעוֹלָם, בּוֹרֵא מִינֵי בְשָׂמִים.

Barukh atah adonai eloheinu melekh ha'olam borei minei v'samim.

Praised are You, Adonai, Sovereign of the Universe, who creates many different kinds of spices.

The leader sniffs the spices and passes the spice box for everyone to share in the fragrant smells.
The leader recites the blessing over the candle.

בָּרוּךְ אַתָּה יהוה אֱלֹהֵינוּ מֶלֶךְ הָעוֹלָם, בּוֹרֵא מְאוֹרֵי הָאֵשׁ.

Barukh atah adonai eloheinu melekh ha'olam borei me'orei ha'eish.

Praised are You, Adonai, Sovereign of the Universe, who creates the lights of the fire.

While the above blessing is recited, family members hold out their hands with palms up, cup their hands, and look at the reflection of the flame on their fingernails. In this way, they make use of the light.

בָּרוּךְ אַתָּה יהוה אֱלֹהֵינוּ מֶלֶךְ הָעוֹלָם, הַמַּבְדִּיל בֵּין קֹדֶשׁ לְחוֹל,
בֵּין אוֹר לְחֹשֶׁךְ, בֵּין יִשְׂרָאֵל לָעַמִּים, בֵּין יוֹם הַשְּׁבִיעִי לְשֵׁשֶׁת יְמֵי
הַמַּעֲשֶׂה. בָּרוּךְ אַתָּה יהוה, הַמַּבְדִּיל בֵּין קֹדֶשׁ לְחוֹל.

Barukh atah adonai eloheinu melekh ha'olam hamavdil bein kodesh l'chol bein or l'choshech bein yisra'eil la'amim bein yom hash'vi'i l'sheishet y'mei hama'aseh. Barukh atah adonai hamavdil bein kodesh l'chol.

Praised are You, Adonai our God, Sovereign of the Universe, who distinguishes between sacred and secular, light and darkness, Israel and other peoples, the seventh day and the six days of labor. Praised are You, Adonai, who distinguishes between sacred and secular.

All take a sip of wine from the Kiddush cup. The leader pours some of the remaining wine onto the plate and puts out the flame of the Havdalah candle. Shabbat has now concluded, and everyone wishes each other shavu'a tov ("a good week").

MAKING FAMILY

Shabbat is primarily a home-oriented celebration, and there are many things that families can do together to prepare for it each week and set the mood during its actual celebration. You may wish to try some of the following suggestions with your own family.

1. Decorate the Shabbat table with fresh flowers or hand-made paper decorations to increase the air of festivity.
2. Put coins in a tzedakah box each week before Shabbat begins. When the box is full, have the family decide together on an appropriate cause to which the money can be donated. We like to empty all the small change from our pockets before putting on our Shabbat clothes.
3. Read Shabbat stories and discuss them as a family.
4. Invite guests to share Shabbat meals with your family. Hospitality has always been an important value in Judaism.
5. Eat at a leisurely and relaxed pace, and always try to include *z'mirot* (Shabbat songs) during your meals.
6. Have someone in your family read a new psalm from the Book of Psalms and briefly discuss it as a family at the beginning of the Friday evening meal.
7. Use your time on Shabbat afternoon to take a nap or read and study Jewish texts like *Pirkei Avot* or *Sefer Hahinnukh*. You may also wish to take a family walk on Shabbat.
8. Bake Shabbat challot as a family project.
9. There are many stimulating and entertaining games that are linked to Shabbat that you can play with your family.

Here is a description of a Bible Charade game:

Purpose
To reenact famous expressions and events in the Bible.

Materials
a. Biblical expressions or events related to the Torah or Haftarah portion of the week.
b. A watch with a second hand for timing the charade.

Imstructions
a. Divide the players into two teams. Give the first player on team 1 the first charade. That player will have two minutes to present nonverbal clues in order to get his/her team to correctly identify the expression or event.
b. If a correct identification is made, that team receives ten points. If no identification is made within the two-minute time limitation, then one point is awarded to the team for each correctly identified word.
c. Present each team in turn with different biblical expressions or events. The team with the most points at the end of a designated number of plays wins.

Note: It is suggested that no expression or event used in this game exceed seven words in length.

Here are some sample charades that can be used with the Torah portion of Genesis (chaps. 1–5):
    a. Adam was created on the sixth day.
    b. On the seventh day God rested.
    c. God said: "Let there be light."
    d. "Am I my brother's keeper?"
    e. Eve gave the apple to Adam.

GLOSSARY

Aliyah. The honor of being called up to the Torah while it is
        being read.
B'samim. The spices used during the Havdalah service.
Birkat Hamazon. The blessing after the meal.
Challah. The twisted loaf eaten on Shabbat and festivals.
Erev Shabbat. Friday, the eve of the Sabbath.

Hamotzi. The blessing over the bread.

Havdalah. "Separation." The service on Saturday night which bids farewell to the Sabbath.

Kabbalat Shabbat. "Welcoming the Sabbath." The prayers immediately preceding the evening service on Friday night.

Kiddush. The blessing over the wine.

N'tilat Yadayim. The ritual washing of hands with a blessing.

Oneg Shabbat. "Sabbath joy." The collation held on Shabbat after prayer services, often including refreshments, song, dance, and discussions.

Se'udah Sh'lishit. The third Sabbath meal, eaten during late Shabbat afternoon.

Shabbat Shalom. "Sabbath Peace," A Shabbat greeting.

Shalom Aleikhem. Hymn welcoming the Sabbath angels.

Rosh Hashanah

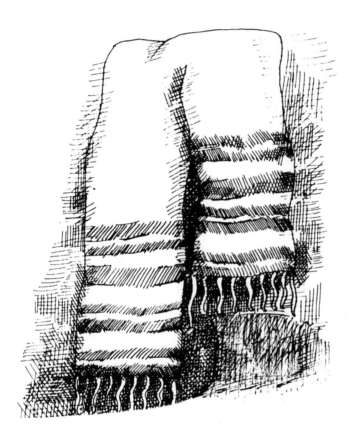

Rosh Hashanah

WORDS OF TORAH

The *Zohar*, the most important book of Jewish mysticism, tells us that Adam, the first human being, was created on Rosh Hashanah. On that day Adam stood before God the Judge; he repented for his mistakes, and God forgave him. God said to Adam: "So it will be with your children. They will stand before me in judgment on Rosh Hashanah, and if they truly say they are sorry, I shall forgive them." Rosh Hashanah is our second chance. It is a time to renew ourselves and resolve to be better people.

BACK TO BASICS

Rosh Hashanah, which means "the head of the year," marks the beginning of the Jewish calendar. It is sometimes called the Birthday of the World, since in Jewish tradition the calendar begins with the story of God's Creation.

Orthodox and Conservative Jews observe Rosh Hashanah for two days, while most Reform and Reconstructionist congregations observe it for one. On Rosh Hashanah Jews believe that God judges us for the coming year. That is why this holiday is also known as Yom Hadin, the Day of Judgment.

In Bible times one of the oldest musical instruments, the shofar (ram's horn), was blown to announce the beginning of the New Year. We remember this custom during the special shofar service on Rosh Hashanah. The shofar serves as our personal alarm clock, awakening us from our sleep and reminding us to consider our past deeds and ask forgiveness for our mistakes.

CALENDAR

Rosh Hashanah falls on the first and second days of the month of Tishri. Interestingly, the Zodiac sign for Tishri is a pair of scales. This is a symbol reminding us that our deeds are weighed and judged in God's Heavenly Book of Life on the New Year.

Despite its name "the beginning of the year," Rosh Hashanah is really is not that, for it comes on the first and second of Tishri, the seventh month of the Jewish calendar.

Many years ago, our ancestors had several different dates which they regarded as new years. Each marked the beginning of an important phase of the year. They counted Nisan, in the spring, as the first month of the year. In this month the Jewish people were freed from Egyptian slavery. The first of Tishri was the beginning of the economic year, the time when the old harvest ended and the new one began. In time, the first of Tishri came to be regarded as the beginning of the year.

The Jewish celebration of Rosh Hashanah has very little in common with the secular celebration on New Year's Eve. The usual secular greeting on New Year's Eve is "Happy New Year," but the traditional Rosh Hashanah greeting is *L'shanah tovah tikateivu* ("May you be inscribed in the Book of Life for a good year"). This reflects the fact that the Jewish New Year is a solemn, serious occasion, not an excuse for merriment. At the same time, it is not an occasion for sadness and gloom. Instead, it is a time to pause for careful consideration of the past year and of the one just beginning. It is an opportunity to think about improving our conduct.

Many important moments in the history of the Jewish people came to be associated with Rosh Hashanah. According to the tradition, Adam was created out of clay on Rosh Hashanah. It was also the birthday of Abraham and Isaac and Jacob, and the day when Moses appeared before Pharaoh. Today many Jewish people like to think of Rosh Hashanah as the birthday of the world itself. However, unlike our own birthdays, this birthday is celebrated with solemnity rather than frivolity.

Elul, the month preceding Rosh Hashanah, has come to be known as the month of preparing for Rosh Hashanah. In the little towns of Eastern Europe, the shammash, or sexton, of the synagogue would march through the streets at daybreak and hammer on the doors and shutters, calling the people to Selichot, the special prayers of forgiveness that were recited during the month of Elul. The shofar is sounded every weekday morning at the close of the service. One belief is that Moses told the Israelites to do so throughout Elul to remind themselves of the sin of the golden calf while he was on Mount Sinai receiving the second set of tablets.

Some people also follow the custom of wishing each other a *shanah tovah* ("good year") either in person or in writing. Many people visit the graves of their loved ones during Elul. In this way they remember those who have deeply affected their lives, thus providing a beautiful transition from the old year to the new.

During the month of Elul, special sections from the books of the prophets, called Haftarot, are read in the synagogue. The basic theme of these sections is consolation and comfort.

The end of the month of Elul is marked by Selichot, the special penitential prayers. It is customary to begin reciting these prayers at twelve o'clock on the Saturday night before Rosh Hashanah. Many synagogues host study sessions preceding these services which set the mood for the holiday.

CELEBRATIONS

In the Synagogue

Rosh Hashanah is primarily a synagogue-oriented festival. Services on this day are considerably longer than usual. The traditional Torah reading for the first day of Rosh Hashanah (Genesis 21) tells about the birth of Isaac to Abraham and Sarah. Tradition has it that it was on Rosh Hashanah that Sarah give birth to Isaac. The Torah reading for the second day of Rosh Hashanah (Genesis 22) tells of the difficult test to which Abraham was subjected when God told him to sacrifice his beloved son Isaac.

The Musaf additional prayers are divided into three parts: *Malkhuyot* ("royalty"), which describes God as the Sovereign One; *Zikhronot* ("remembrance"), which mentions the events that God remembers on Rosh Hashanah; and *Shofarot* ("sounding the ram's horn"), which recalls events connected with the shofar.

Many synagogues today have several Rosh Hashanah services taking place at the same time. In addition to the main service for adults, there may be a service for preschoolers as well as one for teenagers. These services are especially designed to be engaging at the appropriate age levels and often afford opportunity for active participation.

Another special Rosh Hashanah ceremony is the Tashlikh service. During the afternoon on the first day of Rosh Hashanah (or on the second day if the first day is Saturday) it is customary to go to a body of water like a river or lake. Special prayers are recited and the participants throw bread crumbs into the water as a symbol of their desire to cast away their sins and mend their ways.

In the Home
Before Rosh Hashanah begins it is customary to send New Year's cards to friends and relatives. The Hebrew inscription on the cards says *L'shanah tovah tikateivu* ("May you be inscribed for a good year"). On Rosh Hashanah eve the candlelighting blessing and the blessing over the wine are recited. The challot are round instead of the usual long shape to symbolize the hope for an all-around good year. Many families taste a new fruit (one not yet tasted that year) and recite the Shehecheyanu blessing, thanking God for having allowed us to eat this new fruit. It is also customary to eat an apple dipped in honey, symbolizing the promise of a sweet new year.

BASIC BLESSINGS

Candlelighting

בָּרוּךְ אַתָּה יהוה אֱלֹהֵינוּ מֶלֶךְ הָעוֹלָם, אֲשֶׁר קִדְּשָׁנוּ בְּמִצְוֹתָיו וְצִוָּנוּ לְהַדְלִיק נֵר שֶׁל (שַׁבָּת וְשֶׁל) יוֹם טוֹב.

Barukh atah adonai eloheinu melekh ha'olam asher kid'shanu b'mitzvotav v'tzivanu l'hadlik neir (shabbat v'shel) shel yom tov.

Praised are You, Adonai our God, Sovereign of the Universe, who has made us holy by mitzvot and instructed us to kindle the festival candles.

Festival Kiddush

בָּרוּךְ אַתָּה יהוה אֱלֹהֵינוּ מֶלֶךְ הָעוֹלָם, בּוֹרֵא פְּרִי הַגָּפֶן.
בָּרוּךְ אַתָּה יהוה אֱלֹהֵינוּ מֶלֶךְ הָעוֹלָם, אֲשֶׁר בָּחַר בָּנוּ מִכָּל עָם
וְרוֹמְמָנוּ מִכָּל לָשׁוֹן וְקִדְּשָׁנוּ בְּמִצְוֹתָיו. וַתִּתֶּן לָנוּ יהוה אֱלֹהֵינוּ
בְּאַהֲבָה אֶת (יוֹם הַשַּׁבָּת הַזֶּה וְ)אֶת יוֹם הַזִּכָּרוֹן הַזֶּה. יוֹם
(זִכְרוֹן) תְּרוּעָה (בְּאַהֲבָה) מִקְרָא קֹדֶשׁ זֵכֶר לִיצִיאַת מִצְרָיִם. כִּי
בָנוּ בָחַרְתָּ וְאוֹתָנוּ קִדַּשְׁתָּ מִכָּל הָעַמִּים. וּדְבָרְךָ אֱמֶת וְקַיָּם לָעַד.
בָּרוּךְ אַתָּה יהוה מֶלֶךְ עַל כָּל הָאָרֶץ מְקַדֵּשׁ (הַשַּׁבָּת וְ)יִשְׂרָאֵל
וְיוֹם הַזִּכָּרוֹן:

Barukh atah adonai eloheinu melekh ha'olam borei p'ri hagafen. Barukh atah adonai melekh ha'olam asher bachar banu mikol am v'rom'manu mikol lashon v'kid'shanu b'mitzvotav vatiten lanu adonai eloheinu b'ahavah et yom (hashabbat hazeh v'et yom) hazikaron hazeh yom (zikhron) t'ru'ah (b'ahavah) mikra kodesh zeicher litzi'at mitzrayim ki vanu vacharta v'otanu kidashta mikol ha'amim ud'varkha emet v'kayam la'ad. Barukh atah adonai m'kadeish (hashabbat v')yisra'eil v'yom hazikaron.

Praised are You, Adonai, Sovereign of the Universe, who has chosen and distinguished us from all others by adding holiness to our lives with mitzvot. Lovingly you have given us the gift of (this Shabbat and) this Day or Remembrance, a day for (recalling) the sound of the shofar, a day of holy assembly recalling the exodus from Egypt. You have chosen us and endowed us with holiness from among all peoples. Your faithful word endures forever. Praised are You, Adonai, Sovereign of all the earth who hallows (Shabbat and) the people of Israel and the Day of Remembrance.

Shehecheyanu

בָּרוּךְ אַתָּה יהוה אֱלֹהֵינוּ מֶלֶךְ הָעוֹלָם, שֶׁהֶחֱיָנוּ וְקִיְּמָנוּ וְהִגִּיעָנוּ לַזְּמַן הַזֶּה.

Barukh atah adonai eloheinu melekh ha'olam shehecheyanu v'kiymanu v'higi'anu laz'man hazeh.

Praised are You, Adonai our God, Sovereign of the Universe, who has kept us alive, sustained us, and helped us to reach this moment.

On Dipping Applies in Honey

יְהִי רָצוֹן מִלְפָנֶיךָ יְיָ אֱלֹהֵינוּ וֵאלֹהֵי אֲבוֹתֵינוּ שֶׁתְּחַדֵּשׁ עָלֵינוּ שָׁנָה טוֹבָה וּמְתוּקָה.

Y'hi ratzon mil'fanecha adonai eloheinu veilohei avoteinu shet'chadeish aleinu shanah tovah um'tukah.

May it be Your will, Adonai our God and God of our ancestors, to renew for us a new, sweet, and good year.

בָּרוּךְ אַתָּה יהוה אֱלֹהֵינוּ מֶלֶךְ הָעוֹלָם, בּוֹרֵא פְּרִי הָעֵץ.

Barukh atah adonai eloheinu melekh ha'olam borei p'ri ha-etz

Praised are You, Adonai our God, Sovereign of the Universe, who creates of the fruit of the tree.

MAKING FAMILY

Although Rosh Hashanah is primarily a synagogue-oriented holiday, there are many things that families can do together to prepare for the holiday and set the mood. Since Rosh Hashanah has as one of its customs the dipping of apples into honey, many families go apple picking before the holiday. Families that live in communities that have a Tashlikh service will often walk together to the body of water. On arriving there, many families create their own family blessings. For example, they would fill in the following:

1. May God bless you with _____ and _____.
2. May you be _____.
3. May this Rosh Hashanah fill you with _____.

Rosh Hashanah is the festival par excellence for self-examination. Since it is traditional on Rosh Hashanah to review the past year and set new goals for the future, the experiential game called Reflections would be an enjoyable and appropriate family activity.

Each member of the family is given a sheet of paper with the following list of suggested questions. They then take turns sharing their thoughts and answers.

1. What do you really regret doing this past year?
2. What do you really regret *not* doing this past year?
3. What opportunity did you waste last year?
4. Whom do you wish you hadn't hurt this past year?
5. What are your goals for the new year?

Many families enjoy creating their own original Rosh Hashanah greetings cards. Some families also like to create a special birthday card for the world, since Rosh Hashanah is the day on which we celebrate the creation of the world!

GLOSSARY

Avinu Malkeinu. "Our Father, Our King." Well-known High Holy Day prayer.

High Holy Days. Rosh Hashanah and Yom Kippur.

L'shanah tovah tikateivu. "May you be inscribed for a new year."

Machzor. Festival prayerbook.

Malkhuyot. "Royalty." The first of the three divisions of the *Musaf* additional service on Rosh Hashanah.

Musaf. The special additional service.

Rosh Hashanah. "Head of the year."

Shabbat Shuvah. "Sabbath of Repentance." The Sabbath between Rosh Hashanah and Yom Kippur.

Shofar. Ram's horn sounded on Rosh Hashanah.

Shofarot. "Sounding of the shofar." The third of the three divisions of the Rosh Hashanah *Musaf* service.

Sh'varim. Three blasts of the shofar.

Selichot. Prayers of forgiveness recited during the High Holy Days.

Tashlikh. A Rosh Hashanah afternoon service which takes place beside a flowing stream or river.

Ten Days of Repentance. The ten-day period starting on Rosh Hashanah and ending on Yom Kippur. Also called the Days of Awe.

Tishri. The seventh month of the Hebrew year.

Teki'ah. One long blast of the shofar.

T'ki'ah G'dolah. One very long blast of the shofar.

T'ru'ah. Nine quick staccato notes of the shofar.

Yom Hadin. "Day of Judgment." Another name for Rosh Hashanah.

Yom Hazikaron. "Day of Remembrance." Another name for Rosh Hashanah.

Yom T'ru'ah. "Day of Sounding the Horn." The name for Rosh Hashanah as given in the Torah.

Zikhronot. "Remembering." The second of the three divisions of the Rosh Hashanah Musaf service.

Yom Kippur

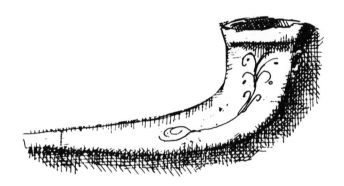

Yom Kippur

WORDS OF TORAH

Yom Kippur has one basic focus: to encourage us, as individuals, to do our part in repairing the world by repairing ourselves. Jewish mystics believe that God actually descends through the spheres of heaven (s'firot) in order to dwell among the people during Yom Kippur. It is at this time, say the mystics, that God is the most accessible. Hence, one appears before God, the Judge of all humanity, in order to atone for the sins of the previous year and commit oneself to better one's life. But first one must "beg m'chilah," ask for the forgiveness of those one has wronged (and in return, it is incumbent upon us to forgive those who ask our forgiveness). Thus, we are taught that "Yom Kippur atones for transgressions against God, but it does not atone for transgressions of one human being against another unless we have made peace with one another" (Mishnah Yoma 8.9).

BACK TO BASICS

The holy day of Yom Kippur originated in the Temple period when special sin offerings (sacrifices) were made in exchange for the atonement (and forgiveness) of the high priest and, through him, of the community. The sins of the community were ceremoniously thrust on a scapegoat which was then sent out into the wilderness to a place designated as Azazel. On this day, the high priest would enter the Holy of Holies (the inner precinct of the Temple) and utter the name of God, something that was not permitted at any other time.

CALENDAR

According to Jewish tradition, one's fate is determined on Rosh Hashanah. We have the opportunity to change the decision during the Ten Days of Repentance and ultimately on Yom Kippur through repentance, tzedakah, and loving deeds of kindness. Yom Kippur, generally considered the holiest day of the year (although technically Shabbat holds that title), is the culmination of the Ten Days of Repentance. Often people speak of Rosh Hashanah–Yom Kippur as one unit rather than distinguishing two holy days. The period, therefore, ends in a special way on the tenth of Tishri, as we are instructed in the Torah: "And it shall be to you a law for all time. In the seventh month, on the tenth day of the month, you shall practice self-denial and you shall do no manner of work, neither the residents nor the visitors that reside among you. This Day of Atonement shall be made for you to cleanse you of all your sins, and you shall be clean before Adonai. It shall be a sabbath of complete rest, and you shall practice self-denial, it is a law for all time" (Leviticus 16:29–31).

In ancient days, in the Jubilee year, the shofar was sounded on the Day of Atonement to indicate the setting free of slaves and the restoration of land to its ancestral owners, in accordance with Leviticus 25:9–10.

While holidays are generally observed for two days in the Diaspora (except in many Reform synagogues), Yom Kippur is exempt. The observance of a two-day fast would be an undue hardship. While the specific timing of Yom Kippur is determined by Rosh Hashanah, it does not occur on Saturday evening since one cannot prepare for Yom Kippur on Shabbat.

In the ancient Temple, courting would take place on Yom Kippur afternoon. Thus, the Torah portion assigned to the afternoon service includes forbidden sexual relationships. In general, the many fertility aspects of the holiday were moved to Sukkot as Yom Kippur became more somber.

OBSERVANCES

Since Yom Kippur is to be a "sabbath of complete rest," the laws of the Sabbath are also enacted for Yom Kippur. Beyond that, the rabbis understood "self-denial" to refer to fasting and a prohibition against wearing leather sandals, anointing the body with oils (cosmetics), bathing for pleasure, and the enjoyment of sexual relations with one's spouse.

In the Synagogue

Services are convened as a court with the Divine Judge sitting in judgment. Normally one may not pray in the company of sinners, but in this context permission to do so is publicly given, since we are all sinners coming to admit our sin as a community of individuals. Evening services begin with the chanting of Kol Nidrei. In the morning service, the cantor actually rises from the midst of the congregation in order to truly be its *sh'liach tzibur* ("messenger").

Yom Kippur is one of the few occasions during which the individual stays in the synagogue throughout the day. Confessional prayers are offered. Synagogue and worshippers are dressed in white to symbolize complete atonement, for "though one's sins are as crimson, they shall be white as snow." Some people wear garments resembling burial-shrouds to emphasize the somber aspect of the day. And a (completely white) tallit (prayer shawl) is worn from the beginning of the evening service through the conclusion of the Ne'ilah service, when the final blast of the shofar is heard.

Other salient aspects of the observance include a litany of forty-two sins at the heart of our confessional; as we recite them, we beat our breasts in contrition. Yom Kippur is the only holy day that has a Haftarah portion in the afternoon. The Yizkor memorial service and the martyrology section of the liturgy identify the observance as well.

In the afternoon, the story of the reluctant prophet Jonah is read.

In the Home
Of the many ways of preparing for the fast and for the opportunity to make atonement for sins, perhaps the most colorful is the ceremony of *kapporot* (or *shluggin kapporos*, as our bubbes and zeydes used to call it). In this ceremony, now no longer widely observed, a chicken (or a fish or even some money) is swirled around the head of a child while these words are spoken: "This is in exchange for you. This is in place of you. This is your atonement. It will go to its death instead of you. But you will go to a good, long life and to peace." The chicken is then taken to the shochet (ritual slaughterer) and given to the poor as tzedakah.

There are no special foods associated with the observance of Yom Kippur, even with the pre-fast dinner. Dairy foods are usually most appropriate for the break-the-fast after Ne'ilah.

A memorial candle is lit in memory of the departed members of the family. In some communities, a similar candle is also lit for the living souls.

Yom Kippur is the only holy day in which men are encouraged to cleanse themselves in the mikveh to fully prepare.

MAKING FAMILY

Since one begins building a sukkah as soon as the fast is over, this is a good time to gather up holiday cards and fasten them together in chains as decorations for the sukkah.

With your kids, make an "I'm Sorry" box. Place it next to the *pushke* (tzedakah box). Ask your kids to think about things they want to be forgiven for but regarding which there is no one to apologize to. Each time they say "I'm Sorry," let them put a coin in the tzedakah box.

BASIC BLESSINGS

While Kiddush is not recited at the start of Yom Kippur, a special candle-lighting blessing is said and children are blessed with the traditional blessing.

בָּרוּךְ אַתָּה יהוה אֱלֹהֵינוּ מֶלֶךְ הָעוֹלָם, אֲשֶׁר קִדְּשָׁנוּ בְּמִצְוֹתָיו וְצִוָּנוּ לְהַדְלִיק נֵר שֶׁל (שַׁבָּת וְשֶׁל) יוֹם הַכִּפּוּרִים.

Barukh atah adonai eloheinu melekh ha'olam, asher kid'shanu b'mitzvotav v'tzivanu l'hadlik neir shel (shabbat v'shel) yom hakippurim.

Praised are You, Adonai our God, Sovereign of the Universe, who has made us holy by mitzvot and instructed us to light the (Shabbat and) Yom Kippur candles.

בָּרוּךְ אַתָּה יהוה אֱלֹהֵינוּ מֶלֶךְ הָעוֹלָם, שֶׁהֶחֱיָנוּ וְקִיְּמָנוּ וְהִגִּיעָנוּ לַזְּמַן הַזֶּה.

Barukh atah adonai eloheinu melekh ha'olam shehecheyanu v'kiymanu v'higi'anu laz'man hazeh.

Praised are You, Sovereign of the Universe, who has kept us alive, sustained us, and helped us to reach this moment.

GLOSSARY

Azazel. The place beyond the wilderness frontier to which the scapegoat was sent, burdened by the sins of the community.

G'mar chatimah tovah. Literally, "May you be sealed well (in the Book of Life)," a greeting used from the end of Rosh Hashanah until the end of Yom Kippur

Kol Nidrei. "All Vows." Prayer which annuls all vows from one Yom Kippur to the next. As a leitmotif it sets the tone at the beginning of the Yom Kippur evening service.

Ne'ilah. The final service of Yom Kippur. The word reflects the notion that the gates of the Temple were about to be closed at this time of day (and thus the opportunity to repent and change the decree was about to expire).

Selichot. Prayers of contrition which along with confessionals color the day.

Shluggin kapporos. Yiddish name for the ceremony in which one twirls a chicken (or fish or money) around one's head in order to project one's sins onto it and send it to its death rather than the individual for his/her sins.

Tzom. Fast.

Yoma. Fifth tractate of the order Moed of the Talmud, a part of which includes laws governing the observance of Yom Kippur.

Yom Hakippurim. Full Hebrew name for the holy day.

Yom Kippur Katan. "Minor Yom Kippur." The eve of each new month, which became a day of fasting and repentance for the pious.

Sukkot

Sukkot

WORDS OF TORAH

"You shall rejoice in your festival (Sukkot) with your son and your daughter. . . . You shall hold the festival for God seven days in the place that God will choose. For God will bless all your crops and all of your undertakings, and you shall have nothing but joy" (Deuteronomy 16:14–15).

Sukkot, the fall harvest and pilgrimage festival, marks the end of the fruit harvest. It is a time of joyous celebration as we thank God for our bounty. We also are reminded of the temporary booths (*sukkot*) which sheltered the Israelites during their wanderings in the wilderness. We commemorate God's redemptive powers by living in our own booths for seven days. Sukkot thus begins the most experiential of all of the Jewish holidays.

BACK TO BASICS

The holiday of Sukkot, called Hechag ("the festival") in the Bible (Leviticus 23:39–40), celebrates both history and nature. After the Israelites were redeemed from Egypt, they wandered in the desert without shelter. The Bible explains that they lived in booths, under God's protection, for forty years. No one knows exactly what the booths looked like. Rabbi Eliezer, an important teacher who lived many centuries ago, described the booths as clouds of God's glory which protected the Israelites from the intense heat of the desert.

When the Jewish people finally reached the Promised Land, they became farmers. During the fall harvest, they built booths near their fields which they often used for protection when harvesting their crops. For this reason the festival of Sukkot is also called Chag Ha'asif, the Festival of the Ingathering. In time, Sukkot became a celebration of both the harvest and the forty years of wandering. The sukkah became an important symbol of protection, and the holiday became a time of feasting and thanksgiving.

CALENDAR

The joyous holiday of Sukkot begins on the eve of the fifteenth of Tishri (in September or early October) and ends nine days later with Simchat Torah. These are days of joy and gladness, and sadness is forbidden. The autumn festival is celebrated in a fragile but well-decorated little house called a sukkah. The Sukkot holiday lasts a total of eight days. The first two days are holy ones when no work is permitted and special prayer services take place in the synagogue. During these days families share festive meals in the sukkah. The next five intermediate days (called Chol Hamo'eid in Hebrew) are celebrated both in the synagogue and in the sukkah. People go to work and school as usual. The last two holy days are Shemini Atzeret and Simchat Torah, which will be described later.

We are instructed to feel joy during this festival of thanksgiving, which in many ways commemorates themes similar to those of the American celebration of Thanksgiving. Many historians believe that the Pilgrims who came to America modeled their own celebration and feast after that of Sukkot, known to them as Tabernacles, which they knew about from reading the Bible.

CELEBRATIONS

In the Synagogue

Services on the first two days of Sukkot include the reading of the Torah portion which describes the sacred seasons of the Jewish year (Leviticus 22:26–23:44). The Hallel service, consisting of psalms of praise to God, is also a part of the Sukkot service.

The Bible designates four plants as essential for the observance of Sukkot: "On the first day you shall take the fruit of goodly trees, branches of palm trees, boughs of leafy trees, and willows of the brook, and you shall rejoice before God seven days" (Leviticus 23:40). In Hebrew these plants are called *arba'ah minim,* the "four species." Each has its own special meaning.

The *lulav* (palm branch), tall and straight, represents the spine. Three sprigs of *hadasim* (myrtle leaves), symbolizing eyes, are tied to the right side of the lulav, and two sprigs of *aravot* (willow leaves), symbolizing the mouth, are tied to the left side of the lulav. The *etrog* (citron), representing the heart, looks like an enlarged lumpy lemon.

The blessing over the lulav is recited each morning immediately before Hallel. The lulav and etrog are waved during key parts of the Hallel service.

The lulav and etrog are used again as a part of a processional. A Torah scroll is marched around the synagogue sanctuary, followed by worshippers bearing *lulavim* and *etrogim*, making a circle around the sanctuary. All sing responsively the Hoshannah prayer, which asks God to save us.

The daily liturgy of the intermediate days of Sukkot is a hybrid. Hallel and the Musaf additional service are included, but the Torah reading is briefer than that of the first two days of the festival.

On a day during Sukkot, usually Shabbat, the Book of Ecclesiastes or parts of it are read. The book is an investigation into the meaning of life. One of its most well known teachings is that there is a time for everything: "To everything there is a season, a time to be born, a time to heal, a time to break down, a time to heal, a time to cry and a time to laugh, a time to keep silent, and a time to speak" (chap. 3).

Hoshannah Rabbah starts on the eve of the seventh day. Its synagogue ritual symbolically reenacts some themes from Yom Kippur. The rabbi and cantor wear white kittels (robes) and the prayers are sung to High Holy Day melodies. There are seven processionals made with the Torah and with the lulav and etrog. This is followed by a reenactment of an ancient Temple ceremony wherein the worshippers took a few dried willow branches in their hands and beat them three times against the ground or a chair until the leaves fell off. Because of the association with Yom Kippur, the beating of the leaves has come to symbolize the shedding of the sins of the past year.

In the Home
It is the custom to begin to build a sukkah immediately following the festival of Yom Kippur. The walls of the sukkah can be made out of any material. The important thing to remember is that the sukkah must have a roof made of s'khakh (leafy branches).

In addition to building the sukkah, you must eat in it. The real mitzvah is to "dwell in the sukkah," however you choose to define this. Since hospitality to others is a religious commandment, it is a wonderful idea to invite guests to one's sukkah. The people you invite will eat the food prepared for the Ushpizin, seven imaginary guests (Abraham, Isaac, Jacob, Joseph, Moses, Aaron, and David) who, according to an ancient mystical tradition, join the family in the sukkah on successive nights of the festival.

On the eve of Sukkot candles are lit in the sukkah and the festival blessing is recited over them. The Kiddush over wine is recited, followed by the special blessing in which we praise God for commanding us to dwell in a sukkah. Then comes the ritual washing of hands and the blessing over the bread. During the meal many families enjoy singing festive songs. The meal concludes with the recitation of the blessing after the meal.

BASIC BLESSINGS

Candlelighting

בָּרוּךְ אַתָּה יהוה אֱלֹהֵינוּ מֶלֶךְ הָעוֹלָם, אֲשֶׁר קִדְּשָׁנוּ בְּמִצְוֹתָיו
וְצִוָּנוּ לְהַדְלִיק נֵר שֶׁל (שַׁבָּת וְשֶׁל) יוֹם טוֹב.

Barukh atah adonai eloheinu melekh ha'olam asher kid'shanu b'mitzvotav v'tzivanu l'hadlik neir shel (shabbat v'shel) yom tov.

Praised are You, Adonai our God, Sovereign of the Universe, who has made us holy by giving us commandments and commanded us to light the (Shabbat and) festival candles.

On Dwelling in the Sukkah

בָּרוּךְ אַתָּה יהוה אֱלֹהֵינוּ מֶלֶךְ הָעוֹלָם, אֲשֶׁר קִדְּשָׁנוּ בְּמִצְוֹתָיו
וְצִוָּנוּ לֵישֵׁב בַּסֻּכָּה.

Barukh atah adonai eloheinu melekh ha'olam asher kid'shanu b'mitzvotav v'tzivanu leisheiv basukkah.

Praised are You, Adonai our God, Sovereign of the Universe, who has made us holy by mitzvot and instructed us to dwell in the sukkah.

Shehecheyanu Prayer for the Gift of Life (first day only)

בָּרוּךְ אַתָּה יהוה אֱלֹהֵינוּ מֶלֶךְ הָעוֹלָם, שֶׁהֶחֱיָנוּ וְקִיְּמָנוּ וְהִגִּיעָנוּ לַזְּמַן הַזֶּה.

Barukh atah adonai eloheinu melekh ha'olam shehecheyanu v'kiymanu v'higi'anu laz'man hazeh.

Praised are You, Adonai our God, Sovereign of the Universe, who has kept us in life, sustained us, and enabled us to reach this festive time.

Festival Kiddush

בָּרוּךְ אַתָּה יהוה אֱלֹהֵינוּ מֶלֶךְ הָעוֹלָם, בּוֹרֵא פְּרִי הַגָּפֶן
בָּרוּךְ אַתָּה יהוה אֱלֹהֵינוּ מֶלֶךְ הָעוֹלָם, אֲשֶׁר בָּחַר בָּנוּ מִכָּל-עָם
וְרוֹמְמָנוּ מִכָּל-לָשׁוֹן, וְקִדְּשָׁנוּ בְּמִצְוֹתָיו. וַתִּתֶּן לָנוּ יהוה אֱלֹהֵינוּ
בְּאַהֲבָה (שַׁבָּתוֹת לִמְנוּחָה וּ)מוֹעֲדִים לְשִׂמְחָה, חַגִּים וּזְמַנִּים לְשָׂשׂוֹן,
אֶת-יוֹם (הַשַּׁבָּת הַזֶּה וְאֶת-יוֹם) חַג הַסֻּכּוֹת הַזֶּה, זְמַן שִׂמְחָתֵנוּ,
(בְּאַהֲבָה) מִקְרָא קֹדֶשׁ, זֵכֶר לִיצִיאַת מִצְרָיִם. כִּי-בָנוּ בָחַרְתָּ וְאוֹתָנוּ
קִדַּשְׁתָּ מִכָּל-הָעַמִּים, (וְשַׁבָּת) וּמוֹעֲדֵי קָדְשֶׁךָ (בְּאַהֲבָה וּבְרָצוֹן)
בְּשִׂמְחָה וּבְשָׂשׂוֹן הִנְחַלְתָּנוּ. בָּרוּךְ אַתָּה יְיָ, מְקַדֵּשׁ (הַשַּׁבָּת וְ)
יִשְׂרָאֵל וְהַזְּמַנִּים.

Barukh atah adonai eloheinu melekh ha'olam, borei p'ri hagafen. Barukh atah adonai eloheinu melekh ha'olam, asher bachar banu mikol am v'ro-m'manu mekol lashon v'kid'shanu b'mitzvotav vatiten lanu adonai eloheinu b'aha-vah (shabbatot lim'nuchah u) mo'adim l'simchah chagim uz'manim l'sasson et yom (hashabbat hazeh v'et yom) chag hasukkot hazeh, z'man simchateinu (b'ahavah) mikra kodesh zeikher litzi'at mitzrayim. Ki vanu vacharta v'otanu kidashta mikol ha'amim (v'shabbat) umo'adei kodsh'kha (b'ahavah uv'ratzon) b'simchah uv'sasson hinchaltanu. Barukh atah adonai, m'kadesh (hashabbat v') yisra'eil v'haz'manim.

Praised are You, Eternal our God, Sovereign of the Universe who creates fruit of the vine.

Praised are You, Eternal our God, Sovereign of the Universe who has chosen and distinguished us from among all others by adding holiness to our lives with mitzvot. Lovingly have You given us (Shabbat for rest,) festivals for joy and holidays for happiness, among them this (Shabbat and this) day of Sukkot, season of our joy, a day of sacred assembly recalling the Exodus from Egypt. Thus You have chosen us, endowing us with holiness from among all peoples by granting us (Shabbat and) Your hallowed festivals (lovingly and gladly) in happiness and joy. Praised are You, God who hallows (Shabbat and) the people Israel and the festivals.

Blessing for Washing Hands

בָּרוּךְ אַתָּה יהוה אֱלֹהֵינוּ מֶלֶךְ הָעוֹלָם, אֲשֶׁר קִדְּשָׁנוּ בְּמִצְוֹתָיו וְצִוָּנוּ עַל נְטִילַת יָדָיִם.

Barukh atah adonai eloheinu melekh ha'olam asher kid'shanu b'mitzvotav v'tzivanu al n'tilat yadayim.

Praised are You, Adonai, Sovereign of the Universe, who has made us holy by mitzvot and instructed us to wash our hands.

Blessing over Bread

בָּרוּךְ אַתָּה יהוה אֱלֹהֵינוּ מֶלֶךְ הָעוֹלָם, הַמוֹצִיא לֶחֶם מִן הָאָרֶץ.

Barukh atah adonai eloheinu melekh ha'olam hamotzi lechem min ha'aretz.

Praised are You, Adonai our God, Sovereign of the Universe, who brings forth bread from the earth.

Birkat Hamazon (Blessing After the Meal)

רַבּוֹתַי נְבָרֵךְ.

Rabotai n'vareikh

Friends, let us give thanks.

The others respond, and the leader repeats:

יְהִי שֵׁם יְיָ מְבֹרָךְ מֵעַתָּה וְעַד עוֹלָם.

Y'hi sheim adonai m'vorakh mei'atah v'ad olam.

May God be praised now and forever.

The leader continues:

בִּרְשׁוּת רַבּוֹתַי, נְבָרֵךְ (אֱלֹהֵינוּ) שֶׁאָכַלְנוּ מִשֶּׁלוֹ.

Bir'shut rabotai n'vareikh (eloheinu) she'akhalnu mishelo.

With your consent friends, let us praise (our God) the One of whose food we have partaken.

The others respond, and the leader repeats:

בָּרוּךְ (אֱלֹהֵינוּ) שֶׁאָכַלְנוּ מִשֶּׁלוֹ וּבטוּבוֹ חָיִינוּ.

Barukh (eloheinu) she'akhalnu mishelo uv'tuvo chayinu.

Praised be (our God) the One whose food we have partaken and by whose goodness we live.

Leader and others:

בָּרוּךְ הוּא וּבָרוּךְ שְׁמוֹ.

Barukh hu uvarukh sh'mo.

Praised be God and praised be God's name.

בָּרוּךְ אַתָּה יהוה אֱלֹהֵינוּ מֶלֶךְ הָעוֹלָם, הַזָּן אֶת הָעוֹלָם כֻּלוֹ בְּטוּבוֹ,
בְּחֵן בְּחֶסֶד וּבְרַחֲמִים. הוּא נוֹתֵן לֶחֶם לְכָל־בָּשָׂר כִּי לְעוֹלָם חַסְדּוֹ.
וּבְטוּבוֹ הַגָּדוֹל תָּמִיד לֹא חָסַר לָנוּ וְאַל יֶחְסַר לָנוּ מָזוֹן לְעוֹלָם
וָעֶד בַּעֲבוּר שְׁמוֹ הַגָּדוֹל, כִּי הוּא אֵל זָן וּמְפַרְנֵס לַכֹּל וּמֵטִיב לַכֹּל
וּמֵכִין מָזוֹן לְכָל־בְּרִיּוֹתָיו אֲשֶׁר בָּרָא. בָּרוּךְ אַתָּה יהוה, הַזָּן אֶת־הַכֹּל.

*Barukh atah adonai, eloheinu melekh ha'olam, hazan et
ha'olam kulo b'tuvo b'chein, b'chesed, uv'rachamim. Hu
notein lechem l'khol basar, ki l'olam chasdo. Uv'tuvo hagadol, tamid lo chasar lanu, v'al yechsar lanu mazon l'olam
va'ed ba'avur sh'mo hagadol, ki hu el zan um'farneis lakol,
umeitiv lakol, umeikhin mazon l'khol b'riyotav asher bara.
Barukh atah adonai, hazan et hakol.*

Praised are You, Eternal, our God, Sovereign of the Universe who sustains the whole world with kindness and compassion. You provide food for every creature, foɪ Your love endures forever. Your great goodness has never failed us. Your great glory assures us nourishment. All life is God's creation and God is good to all, providing every creature with food and sustenance. Praised are You, God who sustains all life.

נוֹדֶה לְךָ יְיָ אֱלֹהֵינוּ עַל שֶׁהִנְחַלְתָּ לַאֲבוֹתֵינוּ אֶרֶץ חֶמְדָּה טוֹבָה וּרְחָבָה, בְּרִית וְתוֹרָה, חַיִּים וּמָזוֹן. יִתְבָּרַךְ שִׁמְךָ בְּפִי כָל־חַי תָּמִיד לְעוֹלָם וָעֶד, כַּכָּתוּב: וְאָכַלְתָּ וְשָׂבַעְתָּ וּבֵרַכְתָּ אֶת־יְיָ אֱלֹהֶיךָ עַל הָאָרֶץ הַטּוֹבָה אֲשֶׁר נָתַן לָךְ. בָּרוּךְ אַתָּה יְיָ, עַל הָאָרֶץ וְעַל הַמָּזוֹן.

Nodeh l'kha adonai eloheinu al shehinchalta la'avoteinu eretz chemdah, tovah ur'chavah, b'rit v'torah, chayim umazon. Yitbarakh shimkha b'fi khol chai tamid l'olam va'ed. Kakatuv v'akhalta v'savata uveirakhta et adonai elohekha al ha'aretz hatovah asher natan lakh. Barukh atah adonai, al ha'aretz v'al hamazon.

We thank you, God, for the pleasing, ample, desirable land which You gave to our ancestors, for the covenant and Torah, for life and sustenance. May You forever be praised by all who live, as it is written in the Torah: "When you have eaten and are satisfied, you shall praise the Eternal your God for the good land which God has given you." Praised are You, God, for the land and for sustenance.

וּבְנֵה יְרוּשָׁלַיִם עִיר הַקֹּדֶשׁ בִּמְהֵרָה בְיָמֵינוּ. בָּרוּךְ אַתָּה יְיָ, בּוֹנֶה בְרַחֲמָיו יְרוּשָׁלָיִם. אָמֵן.

Uv'neih yerushalayim ir hakodesh bimheirah v'yameinu. Barukh atah adonai, boneh v'rachamav yerushalayim. Amen.

Fully rebuild Jerusalem, the holy city, soon in our time.
Praised are You, Adonai, who in mercy rebuilds Jerusalem.
Amen.

בָּרוּךְ אַתָּה יהוה אֱלֹהֵינוּ מֶלֶךְ הָעוֹלָם, הַמֶּלֶךְ הַטּוֹב וְהַמֵּטִיב
לַכֹּל. הוּא הֵטִיב, הוּא מֵטִיב, הוּא יֵיטִיב לָנוּ. הוּא גְמָלָנוּ הוּא
גוֹמְלֵנוּ הוּא יִגְמְלֵנוּ לָעַד חֵן וָחֶסֶד וְרַחֲמִים וִיזַכֵּנוּ לִימוֹת הַמָּשִׁיחַ.

*Barukh atah adonai, eloheinu melekh ha'olam, hamelekh
hatov v'hameitiv lakol. Hu heitiv, hu meitiv, hu yeitiv
lanu. Hu g'malanu, hu gomleinu, hu yigm'leinu la'ad chein
vachesed v'rachamim, vizakeinu limot hamashi'ach.*

Praised are You, God, Sovereign of the Universe who is
good to all, whose goodness is constant through all time.
Favor us with kindness and compassion now and in the
future as in the past. May we be worthy of the days of
the Messiah.

[On Shabbat add:
הָרַחֲמָן, הוּא יַנְחִילֵנוּ יוֹם שֶׁכֻּלוֹ שַׁבָּת וּמְנוּחָה לְחַיֵּי הָעוֹלָמִים.

*Harachaman hu yanchileinu yom shekulo shabbat umenu-
chah l'chayei ha'olamim.*

May the Merciful grant us a day of true shabbat rest,
reflecting the life of eternity.]

[On festivals:
הָרַחֲמָן, הוּא יַנְחִילֵנוּ יוֹם שֶׁכֻּלוֹ טוֹב

Harachaman hu yanchileinu yom shekulo tov.

May the Merciful grant us a day filled with the spirit of the festival.]

וְנִשָׂא בְרָכָה מֵאֵת יְיָ וּצְדָקָה מֵאֱלֹהֵי יִשְׁעֵנוּ וְנִמְצָא חֵן וְשֵׂכֶל טוֹב בְּעֵינֵי אֱלֹהִים וְאָדָם. עֹשֶׂה שָׁלוֹם בִּמְרוֹמָיו הוּא יַעֲשֶׂה שָׁלוֹם עָלֵינוּ וְעַל כָּל־יִשְׂרָאֵל, וְאִמְרוּ אָמֵן.

V'nisa v'rakhah mei'eit adonai utz'dakah mei'elohei yish'einu. V'nimtza chein v'seikhel tov b'einei elohim v'adam. Oseh shalom bimromav hu ya'aseh shalom aleinu v'al kol yisra'eil. V'imru amen.

May we receive blessings from God, loving-kindness from the God of our deliverance. May we find grace and good favor before God and all people. May God who brings peace to the universe bring peace to us and to all the people Israel. And let us say: Amen.

MAKING FAMILY

The holiday of Sukkot is replete with opportunities for families to share and do things together. Here are some suggestions for your family.

1. Build a sukkah together as a family.
2. Collect falling leaves for leaf rubbings and use them to decorate your sukkah, or use your Rosh Hashanah cards as wall hangings in the sukkah.
3. Invite friends to your sukkah with original cards that you design as a family.
4. Take a family nature walk and collect leaves, pine cones, and so forth with which to decorate your sukkah.

5. Visit a pumpkin farm and prepare a pumpkin dish for the holiday.
6. Prepare a huge pot of vegetable soup, involving all the family members in its preparation, including washing, peeling, slicing, and so forth.
7. Make up a list of contemporary heroes, and each night have a different family member invite a new imaginary guest into the sukkah. This activity can be enhanced by having a family member "role play" a contemporary guest. Families members are asked to guess the identity of the contemporary guest.
8. Designate one or several corners of your home or sukkah as the symbolic edge of your field. Use it for the family to collect and place canned goods which will later be donated to a local food bank.
9. Play Sukkot-related games in your sukkah.

GLOSSARY

Aravot. Willow leaves that are attached to the lulav.
Chag. "The Festival." Another name for Sukkot.
Chag Ha'asif. "Feast of Ingathering." Another name for Sukkot.
Chag same'ach. "Happy holiday." A Sukkot greeting.
Etrog. The citron, one of the four species used during Sukkot.
Four Species. The etrog, lulav, aravot, and hadassim.
Hadassim. Myrtle leaves attached to the lulav.
Hoshannot. Prayers said during Sukkot that ask God to save us with God's redeeming powers.
Hoshannah Rabbah. The seventh day of Sukkot.
Lulav. Palm branch, one of the four species.
S'khakh. Leafy greens that are used to make the roof of the sukkah.
Tabernacles. English name for Sukkot, meaning "booths."

Tishri. The Hebrew month in which Sukkot occurs.

Ushpizin. Invisible guests who are invited to visit the sukkah.

Z'man Simchateinu. "Season of Our Joy." Another name for Sukkot.

Shemini Atzeret
and Simchat Torah

Shemini Atzeret
and Simchat Torah

WORDS OF TORAH

Rabbi Joshua ben Levi said: "By rights, Shemini Atzeret should have followed Sukkot after an interval of fifty days, just as Shavuot comes fifty days after Pesach. But since on Shemini Atzeret summer passes into autumn, the time is not suitable for traveling. God was like a ruler who had several married children, some living nearby, while others were a long way away. One day they all came to visit their father. He said, "'Those who live nearby are able to visit me at any time. But those who live at a distance are not able to visit at any time. So while they are all here with me, let us make one big feast for all of them and rejoice with them'" (Song of Songs Rabbah 7:2).

BACK TO BASICS

Shemini Atzeret ("Eighth Solemn Day of Assembly"), the eighth day of Sukkot, is a more somber occasion than the other days of the Sukkot festival. Its most unique feature in synagogue is the prayer for rain in Israel, called Tefillat Geshem in Hebrew. On Shemini Atzeret all other festival observances continue, such as festival candlelighting, holiday foods and clothes, blessings over wine and bread, and a festive atmosphere in the home.

Simchat Torah ("Joy of the Torah"), one of the most joyous of all holidays, comes on the next day. For children and their families, no holiday, with the possible exception of Purim, can compare with this one, which celebrates the conclusion of the cycle of the Torah reading, and includes much merriment, singing, and dancing.

CALENDAR

Shemini Atzeret occurs on the eighth day of Sukkot, which is always the twenty-second of the month of Tishri. Though the festival of Sukkot and Shemini Atzeret are linked together as reasons for rejoicing, there are distinctions between them. For example, the only religious commandment on Shemini Atzeret is that of rejoicing, whereas on Sukkot there are many different mitzvot. In addition, the Sukkot meals take place outside of our homes, whereas on Shemini Atzeret the celebration is in the home.

Simchat Torah occurs immediately following Shemini Atzeret, and marks the occasion of the completion of the reading of the Torah as well as its recommencement. (Some Reform congregations celebrate both on the same day.) Since we conclude the reading of the whole Torah, it is truly an occasion of rejoicing in its honor. Services generally reflect an outburst of joy and celebration. Because of the laughter and gaiety, synagogue sanctuaries are usually filled to capacity with men, women, and children.

CELEBRATIONS

In the Synagogue
As mentioned earlier, a particular feature of Shemini Atzeret is the prayer for rain in Israel, thus officially beginning Israel's rainy season. Since Israel relies so heavily on substantial rain

for its crops, the prayer for rain is recited with a special plaintive melody, and the cantor dons a white kittel (robe), as on Yom Kippur. At the morning service, the Yizkor memorial prayers are recited. The Torah reading (Deuteronomy 14:22–16:17) deals with a variety of laws which Israel must fulfill when settled in its own land. Among them are the tithing of one's produce for the Temple in Jerusalem, the cancelling of loans in the seventh year, called the Sabbatical Year, and a description of the three pilgrimage festivals—Pesach, Shavuot, and Sukkot.

The Simchat Torah service commemorates the conclusion and recommencement of the Torah cycle the reading of the last few verses of the Book of Deuteronomy and immediately beginning again with the first verses from the Book of Genesis. Although the Torah reading could easily be finished in fifteen minutes, it is embellished in song and dance. Members of the congregation, including young children, are given the opportunity of carrying the Torah scrolls around the sanctuary in circuits, called *hakafot*. There are seven circuits around the sanctuary, and as each one is completed, there is singing and dancing with the scrolls before they are handed over to others who will carry them during the next circuit. Children are invited to participate with Simchat Torah flags, original banners, and smaller Torahs. Weather permitting, the circuits and the dancing are often done outdoors, adding to the festiveness of the day.

Following the circuits, all the worshippers are given an opportunity to be called up to the Torah for an aliyah. The aliyot are group ones. Traditionally, the Kohanim (priests) are called first, followed by the Levites and the Israelites (Reform Jews no longer make these distinctions). Each group, standing under a tallit, or prayer shawl, usually held by poles, chants the Torah blessings in unison. The last aliyah, called *kol han'arim*, is reserved for the children. When participants complete their particular aliyah, they are often given a piece of candy as a way of wishing them a sweet year.

The morning services of Simchat Torah also include group aliyot. The final three Torah honors are recited by three honorees called the three grooms, or *chattanim* in Hebrew. These are persons generally known for their dedicated service to the community. The first aliyah goes to the *chattan torah*, the groom of the Torah, whose portion concludes the reading of Deuteronomy. The second aliyah is given to the *chattan B'reishit*, the groom of Genesis, for whom the first chapter of Genesis, the story of creation, is read. Despite the traditional terminology, both women and men may be given these aliyot. As each new day of creation is described, the congregation chants responsively the last few words: "And it was evening and it was morning, the first (second, third . . . sixth) day." The third aliyah is given to the *chattan maftir*, the groom of the reading of the Prophets. On this morning, the prophetic reading (Haftarah) describes Joshua, the leader who took over after Moses. In some congregations it is customary to try to distract the *chattan maftir* during the reading of the Haftarah in various humorous ways. This adds to the frivolity and gaiety of the day.

Simchat Torah thus gives expression to the unbreakable chain—the Torah—which links past and future generations. In that chain lies the secret of the eternal vitality of the Jewish people.

In the Home
The home ritual for Shemini Atzeret and Simchat Torah includes the ritual lighting of candles, the chanting of the festival Kiddush over the wine, ritual handwashing, the blessing over the bread, and the blessing after the meal. On the evening of Shemini Atzeret it is customary before the

candlelighting to light a Yahrzeit memorial candle for each deceased family member.

BASIC BLESSINGS

Candlelighting

בָּרוּךְ אַתָּה יהוה אֱלֹהֵינוּ מֶלֶךְ הָעוֹלָם, אֲשֶׁר קִדְּשָׁנוּ בְּמִצְוֹתָיו וְצִוָּנוּ לְהַדְלִיק נֵר שֶׁל (שַׁבָּת וְשֶׁל) יוֹם טוֹב.

Barukh atah adonai eloheinu melekh ha'olam asher kid'shanu b'mitzvotav v'tzivanu l'hadlik neir shel [shabbat v'shel] yom tov.

Praised are You, Adonai our God, Sovereign of the universe, who has made us holy by mitzvot and instructed us to light the (Shabbat and) festival candles.

Festival Kiddush

בָּרוּךְ אַתָּה יהוה אֱלֹהֵינוּ מֶלֶךְ הָעוֹלָם, בּוֹרֵא פְּרִי הַגָּפֶן. בָּרוּךְ אַתָּה יהוה אֱלֹהֵינוּ מֶלֶךְ הָעוֹלָם, אֲשֶׁר בָּחַר בָּנוּ מִכָּל-עָם וְרוֹמְמָנוּ מִכָּל-לָשׁוֹן, וְקִדְּשָׁנוּ בְּמִצְוֹתָיו. וַתִּתֶּן לָנוּ יהוה אֱלֹהֵינוּ בְּאַהֲבָה (שַׁבָּתוֹת לִמְנוּחָה וּ)מוֹעֲדִים לְשִׂמְחָה, חַגִּים וּזְמַנִּים לְשָׂשׂוֹן אֶת-יוֹם (הַשַּׁבָּת הַזֶּה וְאֶת-יוֹם) הַשְּׁמִינִי חַג הָעֲצֶרֶת הַזֶּה, זְמַן שִׂמְחָתֵנוּ, (בְּאַהֲבָה) מִקְרָא קֹדֶשׁ, זֵכֶר לִיצִיאַת מִצְרָיִם. כִּי-בָנוּ בָחַרְתָּ וְאוֹתָנוּ קִדַּשְׁתָּ מִכָּל-הָעַמִּים, (וְשַׁבָּת) וּמוֹעֲדֵי קָדְשֶׁךָ (בְּאַהֲבָה וּבְרָצוֹן) בְּשִׂמְחָה וּבְשָׂשׂוֹן הִנְחַלְתָּנוּ. בָּרוּךְ אַתָּה יְיָ, מְקַדֵּשׁ (הַשַּׁבָּת וְ) יִשְׂרָאֵל וְהַזְּמַנִּים.

Barukh atah adonai eloheinu melekh ha'olam, borei p'ri hagafen. Barukh atah adonai eloheinu melekh ha'olam, asher bachar banu mikol am v'ro-m'manu mikol lashon v'kid'shanu b'mitzvotav vatiten lanu adonai eloheinu b'aha-vah (shabbatot lim'nuchah u) mo'adim l'simchah chagim

uz'manim l'sasson et yom (hashabbat hazeh v'et yom)
hash'mini chag ha'atzeret hazeh, z'man simchateinu
(b'ahavah) mikra kodesh zeikher litzi'at mitzrayim. Ki vanu
vacharta v'otanu kidashta mikol ha'amim (v'shabbat)
umo'adei kodsh'kha (b'ahavah uv'ratzon) b'simchah uv'sas-
son hinchaltanu. Barukh atah adonai, m'kadesh (hashabbat
v') yisra'eil v'haz'manim.

Praised are You, Eternal our God, Sovereign of the Universe
who creates fruit of the vine.
Praised are You, Eternal our God, Sovereign of the Universe
who has chosen and distinguished us from among all
others by adding holiness to our lives with mitzvot. Lovingly
have You given us (Shabbat for rest,) festivals for joy and
holidays for happiness, among them this (Shabbat and
this) day of Shemini Atzeret, season of our joy, a day of
sacred assembly recalling the Exodus from Egypt. Thus
You have chosen us, endowing us with holiness from
among all peoples by granting us (Shabbat and) Your
hallowed festivals (lovingly and gladly) in happiness and
joy. Praised are You, God who hallows (Shabbat and) the
people Israel and the festivals.

N'tilat Yadayim (Washing the Hands)
Grasp a cup or pitcher of water in your left hand and pour
some over the right. Reverse the process and repeat once or
twice. Recite this blessing:

בָּרוּךְ אַתָּה יהוה אֱלֹהֵינוּ מֶלֶךְ הָעוֹלָם, אֲשֶׁר קִדְּשָׁנוּ בְּמִצְוֹתָיו
וְצִוָּנוּ עַל נְטִילַת יָדָיִם.

Barukh atah adonai eloheinu melekh ha'olam asher
kid'shanu b'mitzvotav v'tzivanu al n'tilat yadayim.

Praised are You, Adonai, Sovereign of the Universe, who has made us holy by mitzvot and instructed us to wash our hands.

Blessing over Bread

בָּרוּךְ אַתָּה יהוה אֱלֹהֵינוּ מֶלֶךְ הָעוֹלָם, הַמּוֹצִיא לֶחֶם מִן הָאָרֶץ.

Barukh atah adonai eloheinu melekh ha'olam hamotzi lechem min ha'aretz.

Praised are You, Adonai our God, Sovereign of the Universe, who brings forth bread from the earth.

Birkat Hamazon (Blessing after the Meal)

רַבּוֹתַי נְבָרֵךְ.

Rabotai n'vareikh

Friends, let us give thanks.

The others respond, and the leader repeats:

יְהִי שֵׁם יְיָ מְבֹרָךְ מֵעַתָּה וְעַד עוֹלָם.

Y'hi sheim adonai m'vorakh mei'atah v'ad olam.

May God be praised now and forever.

The leader continues:

בִּרְשׁוּת רַבּוֹתַי, נְבָרֵךְ (אֱלֹהֵינוּ) שֶׁאָכַלְנוּ מִשֶּׁלּוֹ.

Bir'shut rabotai n'vareikh (eloheinu) she'akhalnu mishelo.

With your consent friends, let us praise (our God) the One of whose food we have partaken.

The others respond, and the leader repeats:

בָּרוּךְ (אֱלֹהֵינוּ) שֶׁאָכַלְנוּ מִשֶּׁלוֹ וּבְטוּבוֹ חָיִינוּ.

Barukh (eloheinu) she'akhalnu mishelo uv'tuvo chayinu.

Praised be (our God) the One whose food we have partaken and by whose goodness we live.

Leader and others:

בָּרוּךְ הוּא וּבָרוּךְ שְׁמוֹ.

Barukh hu uvarukh sh'mo.

Praised be God and praised be God's name.

בָּרוּךְ אַתָּה יהוה אֱלֹהֵינוּ מֶלֶךְ הָעוֹלָם, הַזָּן אֶת הָעוֹלָם כֻּלּוֹ בְּטוּבוֹ, בְּחֵן בְּחֶסֶד וּבְרַחֲמִים. הוּא נוֹתֵן לֶחֶם לְכָל בָּשָׂר כִּי לְעוֹלָם חַסְדּוֹ. וּבְטוּבוֹ הַגָּדוֹל תָּמִיד לֹא חָסַר לָנוּ וְאַל יֶחְסַר לָנוּ מָזוֹן לְעוֹלָם וָעֶד בַּעֲבוּר שְׁמוֹ הַגָּדוֹל, כִּי הוּא אֵל זָן וּמְפַרְנֵס לַכֹּל וּמֵטִיב לַכֹּל וּמֵכִין מָזוֹן לְכָל-בְּרִיּוֹתָיו אֲשֶׁר בָּרָא. בָּרוּךְ אַתָּה יהוה, הַזָּן אֶת-הַכֹּל.

Barukh atah adonai, eloheinu melekh ha'olam, hazan et ha'olam kulo b'tuvo b'chein, b'chesed, uv'rachamim. Hu notein lechem l'khol basar, ki l'olam chasdo. Uv'tuvo hagadol, tamid lo chasar lanu, v'al yechsar lanu mazon l'olam

*va'ed ba'avur sh'mo hagadol, ki hu el zan um'farneis lakol,
umeitiv lakol, umeikhin mazon l'khol b'riyotav asher bara.
Barukh atah adonai, hazan et hakol.*

Praised are You, Eternal, our God, Sovereign of the Universe who sustains the whole world with kindness and compassion. You provide food for every creature, for Your love endures forever. Your great goodness has never failed us. Your great glory assures us nourishment. All life is God's creation and God is good to all, providing every creature with food and sustenance. Praised are You, God who sustains all life.

נוֹדֶה לְךָ יְיָ אֱלֹהֵינוּ עַל שֶׁהִנְחַלְתָּ לַאֲבוֹתֵינוּ אֶרֶץ חֶמְדָּה טוֹבָה
וּרְחָבָה, בְּרִית וְתוֹרָה, חַיִּים וּמָזוֹן. יִתְבָּרַךְ שִׁמְךָ בְּפִי כָל־חַי תָּמִיד
לְעוֹלָם וָעֶד, כַּכָּתוּב: וְאָכַלְתָּ וְשָׂבָעְתָּ וּבֵרַכְתָּ אֶת־יְיָ אֱלֹהֶיךָ עַל
הָאָרֶץ הַטּוֹבָה אֲשֶׁר נָתַן לָךְ. בָּרוּךְ אַתָּה יְיָ, עַל הָאָרֶץ וְעַל
הַמָּזוֹן.

*Nodeh l'kha adonai eloheinu al shehinchalta la'avoteinu
eretz chemdah, tovah ur'chavah, b'rit v'torah, chayim um-
azon. Yitbarakh shimkha b'fi khol chai tamid l'olam va'ed.
Kakatuv v'akhalta v'savata uveirakhta et adonai elohekha
al ha'aretz hatovah asher natan lakh. Barukh atah adonai,
al ha'aretz v'al hamazon.*

We thank you, God, for the pleasing, ample, desirable land which You gave to our ancestors, for the covenant and Torah, for life and sustenance. May You forever be praised by all who live, as it is written in the Torah: "When you have eaten and are satisfied, you shall praise the Eternal your God for the good land which God has given you." Praised are You, God, for the land and for sustenance.

וּבְנֵה יְרוּשָׁלַיִם עִיר הַקֹּדֶשׁ בִּמְהֵרָה בְיָמֵינוּ. בָּרוּךְ אַתָּה יְיָ, בּוֹנֵה בְּרַחֲמָיו יְרוּשָׁלָיִם. אָמֵן.

Uv'neih yerushalayim ir hakodesh bimheirah v'yameinu. Barukh atah adonai, boneh v'rachamav yerushalayim. Amen.

Fully rebuild Jerusalem, the holy city, soon in our time. Praised are You, Adonai, who in mercy rebuilds Jerusalem. Amen.

בָּרוּךְ אַתָּה יהוה אֱלֹהֵינוּ מֶלֶךְ הָעוֹלָם, הַמֶּלֶךְ הַטּוֹב וְהַמֵּטִיב לַכֹּל. הוּא הֵטִיב, הוּא מֵטִיב, הוּא יֵיטִיב לָנוּ. הוּא גְמָלָנוּ הוּא גוֹמְלֵנוּ הוּא יִגְמְלֵנוּ לָעַד חֵן וָחֶסֶד וְרַחֲמִים וִיזַכֵּנוּ לִימוֹת הַמָּשִׁיחַ.

Barukh atah adonai, eloheinu melekh ha'olam, hamelekh hatov v'hameitiv lakol. Hu heitiv, hu meitiv, hu yeitiv lanu. Hu g'malanu, hu gomleinu, hu yigm'leinu la'ad chein vachesed v'rachamim, vizakeinu limot hamashi'ach.

Praised are You, God, Sovereign of the Universe who is good to all, whose goodness is constant through all time. Favor us with kindness and compassion now and in the future as in the past. May we be worthy of the days of the Messiah.

[On Shabbat add:
הָרַחֲמָן, הוּא יַנְחִילֵנוּ יוֹם שֶׁכֻּלּוֹ שַׁבָּת וּמְנוּחָה לְחַיֵּי הָעוֹלָמִים.

Harachaman hu yanchileinu yom shekulo shabbat umenu-chah l'chayei ha'olamim.

May the Merciful grant us a day of true shabbat rest, reflecting the life of eternity.]

[On festivals:

הָרַחֲמָן, הוּא יַנְחִילֵנוּ יוֹם שֶׁכֻּלוֹ טוֹב

Harachaman hu yanchileinu yom shekulo tov.

May the Merciful grant us a day filled with the spirit of the festival.]

וְנִשָׂא בְרָכָה מֵאֵת יְיָ וּצְדָקָה מֵאֱלֹהֵי יִשְׁעֵנוּ וְנִמְצָא חֵן וְשֵׂכֶל טוֹב בְּעֵינֵי אֱלֹהִים וְאָדָם. עֹשֶׂה שָׁלוֹם בִּמְרוֹמָיו הוּא יַעֲשֶׂה שָׁלוֹם עָלֵינוּ וְעַל כָּל־יִשְׂרָאֵל, וְאִמְרוּ אָמֵן.

V'nisa v'rakhah mei'eit adonai utz'dakah mei'elohei yish'einu. V'nimtza chein v'seikhel tov b'einei elohim v'adam. Oseh shalom bimromav hu ya'aseh shalom aleinu v'al kol yisra'eil. V'imru amen.

May we receive blessings from God, loving-kindness from the God of our deliverance. May we find grace and good favor before God and all people. May God who brings peace to the universe bring peace to us and to all the people Israel. And let us say: Amen.

Torah Blessings

בָּרְכוּ אֶת יהוה הַמְּבֹרָךְ:

Bar'chu et adonai ham'vorakh.

Praise Adonai, to whom our praise is due!

בָּרוּךְ יהוה הַמְבֹרָךְ לְעוֹלָם וָעֶד:

Barukh adonai ham'vorakh l'olam va'ed.

Praised be Adonai, to whom our praise is due, now and forever!

בָּרוּךְ אַתָּה יהוה אֱלֹהֵינוּ מֶלֶךְ הָעוֹלָם אֲשֶׁר בָּחַר בָּנוּ מִכָּל הָעַמִּים וְנָתַן לָנוּ אֶת תּוֹרָתוֹ: בָּרוּךְ אַתָּה יהוה נוֹתֵן הַתּוֹרָה:

Barukh atah adonai eloheinu melekh ha'olam asher bachar banu mikol ha'amim v'natan lanu et torato. Barukh atah adonai notein hatorah.

Praised is Adonai our God, Sovereign of the Universe, who has chosen us from among the peoples and given us the Torah. Praised is Adonai, Giver of the Torah.

בָּרוּךְ אַתָּה יהוה אֱלֹהֵינוּ מֶלֶךְ הָעוֹלָם אֲשֶׁר נָתַן לָנוּ תּוֹרַת אֱמֶת וְחַיֵּי עוֹלָם נָטַע בְּתוֹכֵנוּ: בָּרוּךְ אַתָּה יהוה נוֹתֵן הַתּוֹרָה:

Barukh atah adonai eloheinu melekh ha'olam asher natan lanu torat emet v'chayei olam nata b'tokheinu. Barukh atah adonai notein hatorah.

Praised is Adonai our God, Sovereign of the Universe, who has given us a Torah of truth, implanting within us eternal life. Praised is Adonai, Giver of the Torah.

MAKING FAMILY

The following are some suggested activities that families can do together both in preparation for and on Shemini Atzeret and Simchat Torah.

1. Design an original family banner or flag to be used on Simchat Torah in the synagogue.
2. Play Simchat Torah–related games with your family after services. Here is a brief description of Hot Potato, a game that can be played on this festival.

Purpose
To enjoy Hebrew music while manipulating a ball.

Materials
A beachball and a list of Simchat Torah songs.

Imstructions
a. Ask the players to form a circle.
b. Group leader begins to sing a Simchat Torah song while a beachball is quickly passed around the circle from hand to hand.
c. When the singing stops, the player holding the ball is eliminated. The ball then continues to rotate as the music starts again to a new song.
d. The game continues. The last person left in the circle wins and is given the opportunity to be the singer of the songs in the next round.

3. If you have more than one synagogue in your area, you may wish to visit several different synagogue services.
4. Invite some friends to your home to do some Israeli dancing and singing.

5. Bake a cake together as a family and decorate it with a verse from the Bible and a picture to match.

GLOSSARY

Aliyah. Honor of being called to the Torah.

Chattan B'reishit. Special Simchat Torah honor of being called to the Torah for the reading of Genesis.

Chattan Maftir. Special Simchat Torah honor of being called to the Torah for the reading of the Haftarah.

Chattan Torah. Special Simchat Torah honor of being called to the Torah for the reading of the concluding portion of Deuteronomy.

Kittel. White robe worn by the cantor during prayer for rain on Shemini Atzeret.

Kol Hane'arim. "All the children." Special Simchat Torah ceremony of having all children called to the Torah to recite a blessing together.

Tefillat Geshem. Prayer for rain in Israel recited on Shemini Atzeret.

Yahrzeit. Anniversary of one's death, commemorated by lighting a twenty-four-hour candle.

Yizkor. The memorial prayers for the dead.

Hanukkah

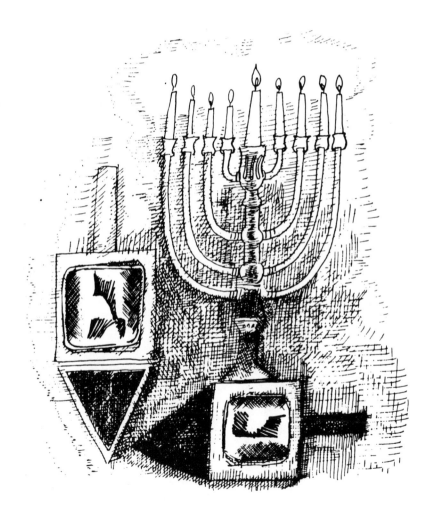

Hanukkah

WORDS OF TORAH

"A Great Miracle Happened *Here*." *Nes Gadol Hayah Poh*. While these words are only found on Israeli dreidels, we believe that the world is too small to speak of *poh* ("here") or *sham* ("there"). The miracle of freedom happened for all of us.

BACK TO BASICS

Hanukkah means "rededication," and it refers to the eight-day rededication of the ancient Temple in Jerusalem, which had been defiled by the Syrian-Greeks in an attempt to totally Hellenize Jerusalem and Israel. Hanukkah is observed for eight days throughout the Jewish world in celebration of this miraculous victory of the spirit. When the rabbis sensed that the military victory of the Maccabees was taking precedence in the minds of the Jewish people, they introduced the notion of the miraculous cruse of oil. According to tradition, the oil burned for eight days—or, at least, the miraculous victory was so great it seemed as if the Temple menorah glowed throughout the eight-day festival of rededication.

CALENDAR

Hanukkah occurs on Kislev 25, which usually comes out in December, around the time of the winter solstice, the darkest day of the year, when we yearn for light.

In the year 165 B.C.E., Judah and a small band of guerilla fighters called the Maccabees forced the Syrian army out of Jerusalem and rededicated the Temple, which had been defiled. Many years earlier, Alexander the Great of Greece had conquered Israel and most of the Near East. When he died in 323 B.C.E., his empire was divided among his generals, two of whom established kingdoms of their own in Egypt and Syria. Israel, located between these countries, was valuable to both and became a political pawn (and battlefield), sometimes ruled by one and sometimes by the other.

In 175 B.C.E., when Israel was under Syrian control, Antiochus IV (Antiochus Epiphanes) became king of Syria. In an effort to strengthen his hold on Israel, he decreed that all of his subjects must worship the same (Greek) gods and follow the same (Greek) customs. The Jews were not permitted to study Torah, keep Shabbat, or do anything Jewish.

Some Jews, called Hellenists, liked the Greek way of life. They wore Greek clothing and spoke the Greek language. Others, their opponents, called the Hasidim (not to be confused with the modern Hasidim known by their black coats, fur hats, and *pei'ot*), did not approve of Hellenization. They felt that the influence of Greek culture would destroy Judaism. The Hasidim began their opposition with a simple refusal to obey the laws of Antiochus. As a result, they suffered harshly. Thus, there was no choice but to rebel. Beginning in the small town of Modiin, not far from Jerusalem, a priest named Mattathias started the revolt. He called on others to join him: "Whoever is for God, come with me." The small band of Mattathias and his five sons began a guerilla offensive in the hills against the mighty Syrian-Greek army. Led by one of the sons, Judah ha-Maccabee, this small army liberated Jerusalem. This indeed was a miraculous victory.

They cleansed the Temple, removed the statues of Zeus and other Greek gods. And on the twenty-fifth day of Kislev in the year 165 B.C.E., they rededicated the Temple. Following the model of Sukkot, which they had not been able to celebrate, the dedication of the Temple lasted for eight days. Slowly, the aspects of the Sukkot celebration in the context of Hanukkah gave way to particular events reserved for Hanukkah only.

CELEBRATIONS

In the Synagogue
Historically, because of the pride engendered by the Maccabean defeat of the Syrian-Greeks, celebrations of Hanukkah focused on the military victory. In response to this, the rabbis emphasized that the victory was only possible because the Maccabean freedom-fighters were motivated by religious faith. To drive this home, they selected as the Haftarah for Shabbat Hanukkah a reading from the prophet Zechariah: "Not by might and not by power, but by My spirit, says Adonai" (Zechariah 4:6). To further defuse the military victory, they also told the story of the miracle of the oil.

While candles are usually lit at home, the liturgy in the synagogue reflects the ambience of Hanukkah. Hallel is recited, and the melody of Ma'oz Tzur influences the nusach (melody) of certain prayers.

In the Home
Lighting candles. Light is a symbol associated with nearly all Jewish holy days and festivals. The Hanukkah lights mark each day of the festival and are reminders of the menorah which burned in the ancient Temple. Using a helper candle (shammash) to light them, eight candles are lit in a hanukkiyah (Hanukkah menorah/candle holder), starting with one on the first day and adding another each additional day so that

eight candles are burning on day eight. Remember: load your candles from the right; light from the left, starting with the newest candle.

Playing dreidel. Probably based on a German gambling game, this game was designed to emphasize the miracle of Hanukkah. Thus each of the four sides of the dreidel is marked with a Hebrew letter standing for the phase *Nes Gadol Hayah Sham* ("A Great Miracle Happened There").

Taking turns, one person spins at a time. Winning or losing is determined by which side of the dreidel is facing up when it falls. Nun stands for "nothing" (*nisht* in Yiddish), so the player does nothing. Gimmel stands for "all" (*gantz* in Yiddish), so the player takes everything in the pot. Heh stands for "half" (*halb* in Yiddish), so the player takes half of what is in the pot. Shin stands for "put in" (*shtel* in Yiddish), so the player puts one in the pot.

Eating latkes and sufganiyot. Since the miracle legend is associated with oil, various traditions developed regarding the eating of foods made with oil. In the Ashkenazic communities, potato pancakes (latkes) became the favorite. In many Sephardic families, jelly doughnuts (sufganiyot) fried in oil became the festival food of choice.

MAKING FAMILY

1. Plan a torch run around your block. Like a relay race, go once around for each night with different runners, all lit by the shammash stationed in front of your house. Invite your neighbors to participate.
2. Build a giant hanukkiyah on your front lawn. If it gets really cold, carve one out of ice and make an ice sculpture.

3. Invite your neighbors and have a latke-eating or latke-cooking contest.
4. Play Hanukkah-oriented family games.

a. Pin the Candles on the Hanukkiyah

Materials. A 2 foot by 2 foot papercut hanukkiyah with paper candles approximately 6 inches in length. Cover the hanukkiyah's back side with felt, and attach a piece of felt to the backs of each of the paper candles.

Instructions. Each family member is given a candle and is blindfolded. Players, in turn, try to append their candles to the wicks of the hanukkiyah. The players with candles closest to the wicks win.

b. The Dancing Doughnuts Game

Materials. Have the players sit in a line. Tie a piece of string across the room at the approximate height of their heads. To that string tie a number of shorter pieces of string, and to each of them tie a sugar-covered doughnut which should extend to the lips of the players.

Instructions. Each player is required to eat the doughnut angling before him or her without using hands. While the players wrestle with their doughnuts, a family member moves the horizontal string. The result will be seen on the sugar-coated faces of the players when the game is over.

5. Make potato latkes.
   3 large potatoes (2 cups grated)
   1 small onion
   2 eggs (egg whites for the cholesterol conscious)
   2 tablespoons flour or matzah meal
   1 teaspoon salt

Grate potatoes and place them in a bowl. Grate in the onion. Add eggs, flour, and salt. Drain off excess liquid. Drop by spoonfuls into well-oiled frying pan. Fry on both sides in hot oil. Serve with apple sauce or sour cream.

No Peel Latkes
>1 egg
>1 small onion cut into quarters
>3 cups of unpeeled potatoes, cut into cubes
>2 tablespoons flour
>1 tablespoon oil
>¼ teaspoon sugar
>½ teaspoon salt
>⅛ teaspoon pepper

Blend the egg and onion for a few seconds in a blender. Add half the potatoes. Blend until smooth. Add the other ingredients. Blend until smooth. Drop by spoonfuls into a well-oiled frying pan. Fry on both sides. Drain on a paper towel. Serve with apple sauce or sour cream.

6. Make Sufganiyot.
>¾ cup orange juice or water
>¼ pound margarine
>4 tablespoons sugar
>2 packages dry yeast
>3 cups flour
>2 eggs, beaten
>dash of salt

Combine orange juice, margarine, and sugar, and heat until margarine melts. Cool to lukewarm and add yeast. Stir until dissolved. Combine all ingredients and mix. Knead until smooth. (You may need to add more flour.) Place dough in greased bowl and cover. Let rise in a warm spot for a half-hour. Punch down. Shape small pieces of dough into balls, rings, or twists. Cover and let rise another half-hour. Deep fry in hot oil. Drain. Put a few teaspoons of powered sugar or cinnamon in a paper bag. Add doughnuts and shake.

BASIC BLESSINGS

On lighting the Hanukkiyah
(on each night)

בָּרוּךְ אַתָּה יהוה אֱלֹהֵינוּ מֶלֶךְ הָעוֹלָם, אֲשֶׁר קִדְּשָׁנוּ בְּמִצְוֹתָיו וְצִוָּנוּ לְהַדְלִיק נֵר שֶׁל חֲנֻכָּה.

Barukh atah adonai eloheinu melekh ha'olam asher kid'sha-nu b'mitzvotav v'tzivanu l'hadlik neir shel chanukkah.

Praised are You, Adonai our God, Sovereign of the Universe, who has made us holy by mitzvot and instructed us to light the Hanukkah candles.

(on each night)

בָּרוּךְ אַתָּה יהוה אֱלֹהֵינוּ מֶלֶךְ הָעוֹלָם, שֶׁעָשָׂה נִסִּים לַאֲבוֹתֵינוּ בַּיָּמִים הָהֵם וּבַזְּמַן הַזֶּה.

Barukh atah adonai eloheinu melekh ha'olam, she'asah nissim la'avoteinu bayamim haheim uvaz'man hazeh.

Praised are You, Adonai our God, Sovereign of the Universe, who performed miracles for our ancestors at this season in ancient days.

(on first night only)

בָּרוּךְ אַתָּה יהוה אֱלֹהֵינוּ מֶלֶךְ הָעוֹלָם, שֶׁהֶחֱיָנוּ וְקִיְּמָנוּ וְהִגִּיעָנוּ
לַזְּמַן הַזֶּה.

*Barukh atah adonai eloheinu melekh ha'olam sheheche-
yanu v'kiymanu v'higi'anu laz'man hazeh.*

Praised are You, Adonai our God, Sovereign of the
Universe, who has given us life, sustained us, and helped
us to reach this moment.

Following the lighting of the candles, the Hanerot Hallalu is
recited. Remember to include the Al Hanissim section (a
summary of the event) during the reciting of the Amidah and
in the Blessing After the Meal. Don't forget to read the Hallel
psalms during the eight days.

GLOSSARY

Dreidel. Spinning top (Hebrew, *sevivon*).
Hanukkiyah, Candle holder or menorah specifically for
    Hanukkah.
Hasidim. Religious purists (opponents of the Hellenizers).
Latkes. Potato pancakes (Hebrew, *levivot*).
Maccabees. Guerilla fighters who fought the Syrian Greeks in
    165 B.C.E.
Neir. Candle.
Nes Gadol Hayah Poh/Sham. "A Great Miracle Happened
    Here/There." Inscription on the dreidel.
Shammash. Helper candle used to light candles in the
    hanukkiyah.
Sufganiyot. Jelly doughnuts.

Tu Bishevat

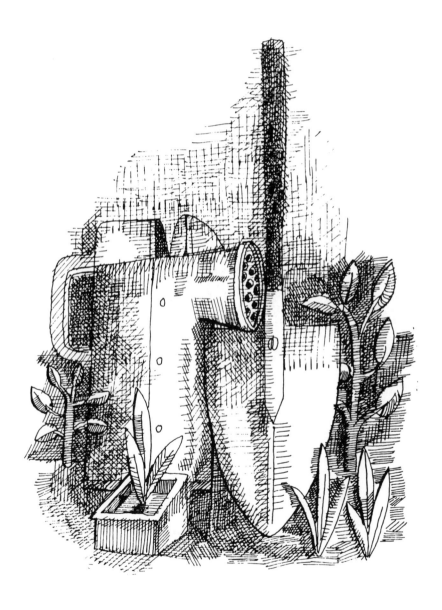

Tu Bishevat

WORDS OF TORAH

Tu Bishevat offers us a stepping stone to spring. As the sap begins to flow again and bring the trees to life, we all feel renewed by the promise of spring. Thus, the awakening of a tree's life is to be observed, for trees represent hope for the future. Rabbi Yochanan ben Zakkai taught his students: "If you are planting a tree and you see the Messiah coming . . . finish planting the tree and then go greet the Messiah."

BACK TO BASICS

In a special way, Tu Bishevat celebrates both the Creator and the creation. Psalm 104, one of the psalms traditionally recited on Tu Bishevat, expresses this sentiment rather well:
   The trees of Adonai have their fill;
   The cedars of Lebanon, which You planted,
   Where the birds make their nests;
   As for the stork, the fir trees are her house.
The mystical influence is also felt during the celebration because the heavenly spheres are often illustrated in the form of a tree. Saying blessings over the various species is said to release the sparks of life in the fruits.
   Almond trees are best associated with Tu Bishevat since they are usually the first trees to blossom in Israel, filling the air with their fragrance.

CALENDAR

According to the Mishnah (Rosh Hashanah 1:1), the fifteenth of Shevat was the cutoff date for determining when the fruit of the tree was to be tithed. The fruit of a tree which matured prior to this date was to be counted toward the previous year. After that date, it was part of next year's tithing. Thus, Tu (for *tet-vav*, from the alpha-numerical expression of the number 15) Bishevat became the festival of the trees, or literally the "new year" of the trees. The date was chosen because the night of the fifteenth is bathed in the light of the full moon rather than the new moon at the beginning of the month. Most of the rain has fallen in Israel by the month of Shevat and the trees begin to drink from it. As a result, their sap begins to flow.

CELEBRATIONS

Since the center of our world is Jerusalem (Israel), we celebrate the birth of spring there by planting saplings and eating the fruits of its season: "A land of wheat and barley, of vines, figs, and pomegranates, a land of olive oil and [date]-honey" (Deuteronomy 8:8).

In the Synagogue

This is the time of year that funds are collected to plant trees in Israel and also to invest in other projects there supported by the Jewish National Fund (which collects coins in the well-known blue boxes).

Ashkenazi Jews recite Psalm 24 and the Psalms of Ascent (Psalms 120–134), associating these fifteen psalms with fifteen kinds of fruits and with the fifteenth of Shevat. Sephardi Jews often stay up all night studying passages reflecting agriculture in the land of Israel.

In the Home
A Tu Bishevat Seder (sometimes called *chemdat hayamim*, "meals made from the fruits of the season") is the traditional way to celebrate this festival. The kabbalists of Safed began the tradition of four cups of wine (white wine, white mixed with a little red, red mixed with a little white, and all red wine) to reflect the change of the seasons. Since there is no fixed liturgy, only a mix of community customs, it is a good opportunity to be creative.

MAKING FAMILY

1. With your family, try to think of all the things that trees do for us. Trees give us fruits and nuts. Furniture and paper are made from trees. Chemicals from the bark and leaves of many trees are used in medicine, paint, floor wax, plastic, soap, shoe polish, and chewing gum. Trees give off oxygen which we need to breathe. Shade trees keep us cool and protect us from strong winds. Trees are homes for birds and small animals, and, of course, wood is used to build many of our homes.

2. At Kibbutz Hafetz Hayyim, hydroponics have been used for the last thirty-five years to grow vegetables. In the Torah (Exodus 15:2–11) it says: "During the seventh year, you shall let it [your land] lie fallow." The rabbis of Israel have agreed that since the seventh year, the *sh'mittah*, or sabbatical, year, is a rest for the soil, crops may be grown in water. So Hafetz Hayyim can continue to grow vegetables during the sabbatical year. Try it yourself.

    a. Put small pebbles or aquarium gravel in a container.

    b. Add enough water to cover the gravel.

    c. Carefully put seedlings in the water. Be sure to wash off any soil from the root.

    d. Space seedlings about 2 ½ inches apart.

    e. Mix hydroponic plant food and add to the water.

    f. Put container near a sunny window.

    g. Add water to keep pebbles covered.

3. As a family, buy JNF tree certificates. Together, decide whom to honor.

4. Go tree sapping. (You can call your local county environmentalist for advice on where you can do this in your area.)

5. Make an ecology pact to be signed by family members. In this pact, you can include agreements concerning recycling and other matters pertaining to ecology and the preservation of the earth.

BASIC BLESSINGS

Over Wine

בָּרוּךְ אַתָּה יהוה אֱלֹהֵינוּ מֶלֶךְ הָעוֹלָם, בּוֹרֵא פְּרִי הַגָּפֶן.

Barukh atah adonai eloheinu melekh ha'olam borei p'ri ha-gafen

Praised are You, Adonai our God, Sovereign of the Universe, who creates of the fruit of the vine.

Over Each New Fruit

בָּרוּךְ אַתָּה יהוה אֱלֹהֵינוּ מֶלֶךְ הָעוֹלָם, בּוֹרֵא פְּרִי הָעֵץ.

Barukh atah adonai eloheinu melekh ha'olam borei p'ri ha-etz

Praised are You, Adonai our God, Sovereign of the Universe, who creates of the fruit of the tree.

Over a Fruit Eaten for the First Time That Year

בָּרוּךְ אַתָּה יהוה אֱלֹהֵינוּ מֶלֶךְ הָעוֹלָם, שֶׁהֶחֱיָנוּ וְקִיְּמָנוּ וְהִגִּיעָנוּ לַזְּמַן הַזֶּה.

Barukh atah adonai eloheinu melekh ha'olam shehecheyanu v'kiymanu v'higi'anu laz'man hazeh.

Praised are You, Adonai our God, Sovereign of the Universe, who has kept us alive, sustained us, and helped us to reach this moment.

GLOSSARY

Bal tashchit. Literally "do not destroy," the rabbinic ethic of protecting nature, which stems from the Torah command not to destroy trees in time of war (Deuteronomy 20:19).

Bokser. Carob, the fruit said to have been eaten by Shimon bar Yochai during the years he hid in a cave from the Romans.

Bolsa de frutas. "Bag of fruit" distributed to children by Sephardi Jews.

Chag Ha'ilanot. "Festival of Trees." Another name for Tu Bishevat.

Chag Hapeirot. "Festival of Fruits." Another alternative name for Tu Bishevat.

Chamishah Asar Bishevat. "Fifteenth of Shevat." Another name for Tu Bishevat.

Complas. Special poems recited by Sephardi Jews during the Tu Bishevat Seder.

Ma'ot peirot. "Fruit money," charity distributed by Sephardi Jews similar to the "wheat money" of Pesach.

Purim

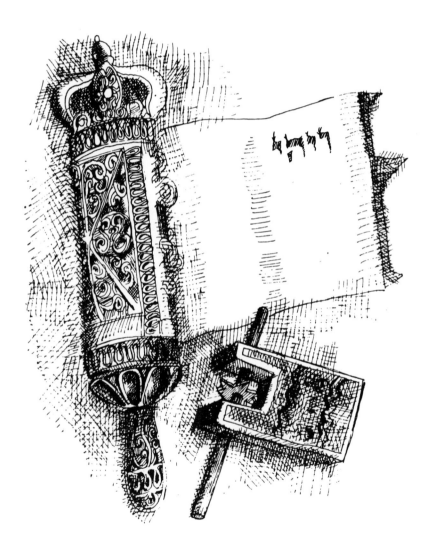

Purim

WORDS OF TORAH

"On Purim," says a Jewish proverb, "everything is permissible." Purim is the one time of year when the normal rules of behavior are suspended somewhat, when even the most devout Jews dare to make a mockery of things that are normally considered sacred. But Jewish piety is a balance, a mix of the spiritual and the physical. It is out of this context that the Purim celebration is born. But remember, "Be Happy. It's Adar."

BACK TO BASICS

The festival of Purim celebrates the successful overthrow of a plot to destroy the Jews of ancient Persia. Its establishment as a feast is recounted in Esther 9:20–28. The name Purim is said to come from the word for the "lots" or "marked stones" which Haman, the villain in the story, uses to arbitrarily pick the date on which he intends to annihilate the Persian Jewish community. While there is some scholarly debate about the historical veracity of what is accounted in Megillat Esther, the essential message of survival rings true for Jews in all generations, including our own.

CALENDAR

Purim is celebrated on the 14th of Adar, the day following the one on which Haman intended to destroy the Jews.

Instead, the king hanged Haman and allowed the Jews of Persia to defend themselves. The Jews of Shushan, the capital, celebrated on the fifteenth of Adar because they fought back for two days. This day has become known as Shushan Purim. Out of respect for Jerusalem, all cities that have walls (as did Shushan) celebrate Purim on the same day (according to Mishnah Megillah 1:1). In a leap year Purim is celebrated in Adar II, the extra month added to the calendar. (The corresponding date for Purim in Adar I during a leap year is referred to as Purim Katan.)

The Purim story takes place in ancient Persia (modern Iran) around the fifth century B.C.E. In Shushan, its capital, King Ahasuerus expelled Queen Vashti for her refusal to dance before his friends during a six-month-long party (and extended week-long banquet) celebrating the third year of his reign. Mordecai, a local scribe (and therefore a nobleman), encouraged his niece Esther, whom he had raised, to join the king's harem and strive to become his queen.

Some years later, Mordecai was instrumental in saving the king's life. He had overheard a plot to poison the king's wine. While it was Mordecai who provided the information through Esther, it was Haman, one of the king's ministers, who was charged with investigating the rumor. Haman's success in uncovering the plot led the king to appoint him to the post of prime minister.

Now second in authority only to the king, and filled with pride, Haman wanted people to bow down to him. When Mordecai refused, Haman vowed to kill him and all the Jews of Persia along with him. He sought the advice of a fortune teller, who used marked stones (*purim*) to determine the month and day on which they should die. Haman obtained the king's permission to destroy the Jewish community, but then Esther intervened. In the end, Haman was hanged on the gallows which he had prepared for Haman, and the Jews of Persia were given permission to defend themselves against the decree that the king had signed against them.

Following the pattern of the Purim in the Bible, there are also local Purim celebrations in some communities on other dates. These commemorate occasions when these communities, like the Jewry of Persia, were rescued from destruction and annihilation.

CELEBRATIONS

The frivolous, masquerade-like celebration of Purim presents the parent with some real challenges. Some of the "values" reflected in the celebration of Purim may seem inappropriate unless they are examined carefully and placed in a proper context. For example, Vashti's refusal to dance for the king's drunken friends was an act of personal courage, not insubordination, as the biblical text suggests. She was not chattel; yet the king treated her as such. And the competition, euphemistically referred to as a beauty contest, that Esther entered was one which suggests that women are to be appreciated for their "beauty" alone—something that we have eschewed in the contemporary Jewish community. Finally, the celebration of Haman's utter destruction (which included the death of his children and their families, so as to totally destroy his seed) is certainly not something to be used as a model for moral living.

In the Synagogue

The Megillah (a small scroll on which the Book of Esther is inscribed) is read with special cantillations at the festival evening and morning services. The scroll is spread out and read like a letter. The four verses which speak of the redemption of the Jews of Shushan are read in a louder voice. And to blot out the memory of Amalek (following the instruction of Deuteronomy 25:19), thunderous noises are made whenever Haman's name is mentioned. Other traditions regarding the reading of the Megillah include the recitation of the names of all ten sons of Haman in one breath to show their simultaneous execution. (This is also explained as a refusal by Jews to gloat over the downfall of their enemies—in order to do so, they get through the reading quickly.)

It is an old custom that every person give a half-shekel (a small Hebrew coin) for the poor, just prior to the reading of the Megillah.

In the Home
There are many special foods associated with Purim, often with different names. These foods have generally been drawn from the details of the Purim story, as have the other celebrations associated with the festival. A festive evening meal is generally the common thread that binds together all of the different activities in the home.

BASIC BLESSINGS

בָּרוּךְ אַתָּה יהוה, אֱלֹהֵינוּ מֶלֶךְ הָעוֹלָם אֲשֶׁר קִדְּשָׁנוּ בְּמִצְוֹתָיו,
וְצִוָּנוּ עַל־מִקְרָא מְגִלָּה:

Barukh atah adonai eloheinu melekh ha'olam asher kid'shanu b'mitzvotav v'tzivanu al mikra megillah.

Praised are You, Adonai our God, Sovereign of the Universe, who made us holy by mitzvot and instructed us to read the Megillah.

בָּרוּךְ אַתָּה יהוה, אֱלֹהֵנוּ מֶלֶךְ הָעוֹלָם, שֶׁעָשָׂה נִסִּים לַאֲבוֹתֵנוּ,
בַּיָּמִים הָהֵם, בַּזְּמַן הַזֶּה:

Barukh atah adonai eloheinu melekh ha'olam she'asah nisim lavoteinu bayamim haheim bazman hazeh.

Praised are You, Adonai our God, Sovereign of the Universe, who performed miracles for our ancestors at this season in ancient days.

בָּרוּךְ אַתָּה יהוה אֱלֹהֵינוּ מֶלֶךְ הָעוֹלָם, שֶׁהֶחֱיָנוּ וְקִיְּמָנוּ וְהִגִּיעָנוּ
לַזְּמַן הַזֶּה.

Barukh atah adonai eloheinu melekh ha'olam sheheche-yanu v'kiymanu v'higi'anu laz'man hazeh.

Praised are You, Adonai our God, Sovereign of the Universe, who has given us life, sustained us, and helped us to reach this moment.

MAKING FAMILY

Easy Costumes
1. Use a half-slip for Queen Esther. Pull it up under your arms and add ribbon for straps.
2. Use an old dress for a slightly larger Queen Esther.
3. A bathrobe or an old shirt is great for Mordecai, Ahasuerus, or Haman. Just add a belt.
4. Fancy pajamas, Mom or Dad's, are great for any Purim character.
5. Costume jewelry adds to any costume.

6. Crowns can be made from cut cardboard wrapped with aluminum foil. Use glitter or spray-painted macaroni to add that special touch.

Hamantaschen
This recipe, our family's own, is guaranteed to make the very best hamantaschen.

> 1 pound vegetable shortening
> 5 cups flour
> 1 teaspoon salt
> 1 cup pineapple juice
> ½ cup sugar

Mix and refrigerate roll of sugared flour. Cut and fill. Bake at 400 degrees for 20–25 minutes.

> Cream Cheese Filling
> ¾ cup brown sugar
> 3 ounces cream cheese
> ½ teaspoon salt (we don't use)
> 1 teaspoon vanilla
> ½ cup either nuts, chocolate chips (our favorite), coconut, or brickle

Best if chilled. Mix all ingredients. Fill dough and bake.

Packing for Shushan
The Packing for Shushan game will help family members share their knowledge of Purim with one another. Here are the instructions:
a. One person begins by saying, "I pack my trunk with a Purim costume." The next player, "I pack my trunk with a Purim costume and a gregger." The third person must repeat

the first two objects and add an additional one, such as, "I pack my trunk with a Purim costume and a gregger and a mask." Each person repeats all of the items previously mentioned in order and adds a new one.

b. A player who fails to correctly repeat the list is eliminated from the game. The game continues until the contents of the trunk are too numerous to remember.

GLOSSARY

Adloyadah. Purim party; from the Hebrew phrase *ad lo yadah,* literally "until one does not know," referring to the questionable practice of drinking until one does not know the difference between "Blessed be Mordecai" and "Cursed be Haman."

Hamantaschen. Purim pastry, said to resemble Haman's three-cornered hat. Alternatively, *oznai-Haman* ("Haman's ears") in Hebrew.

Megillah. "Scroll." Specifically, Megillat Esther, or the Scroll of Esther, the biblical book which recounts the story of Purim. Also the name of a tractate of the Talmud which includes the details of the observance of Purim.

Matanot la'evyonim. "Gifts to the poor," mandated as part of the observance of Purim.

Purimspiel. Play or parody on the Purim story, either as a monologue or group performance, originally presented during the festival meal but now generally presented in public as part of the Purim festivities.

Purim se'udah. Purim feast.

Ra'ashan. "Noisemaker" (Hebrew); alternatively, *gregger* (Yiddish).

Shelakhmones. Gifts of fruit and pastry to friends, reflective of the tradition of giving gifts to the poor (*mishlo'ach manot*).

Ta'anit Esther. "Esther's fast." Occurs on the day before Purim, commemorating the fast of Esther before she went to Ahasuerus to plead for the life of the Jews of Persia.

Pesach

Pesach

WORDS OF TORAH

One of the oldest and most colorful and dramatic of all of our festivals is Pesach (Passover), which celebrates the liberation of Israel from Egyptian slavery. It is the national birthday of the Jewish people, and its many laws and regulations have been observed in many different ways for centuries. The Torah says repeatedly, "Remember, you were slaves in Egypt." It is remarkable how well we have remembered and continue to commemorate our development from slavery to life as a free people.

BACK TO BASICS

The English name "Passover" is a literal translation of one of the two biblical names for the festival of Pesach. The Hebrew term *pesach*, which means to "pass over," reminds us of the special Divine protection which the Israelites enjoyed in Egypt during the tenth plague, when the angel of God passed over their houses while slaying every Egyptian firstborn male. The other biblical name for this holiday, Chag Hamatzot ("Festival of Unleavened Bread"), serves to remind us of the unleavened bread which the Israelites hastily made when they hurriedly left Egypt and had no time to let their dough rise. The eating of unleavened bread (matzah) is one of the most important Pesach observances to this day.

In our prayerbook liturgy, Pesach is called Z'man Cheiruteinu ("Season of Our Freedom"), marking our liberation from Egyptian bondage and our new beginning as a free and independent people. From now on the Israelites were not just a band of twelve loosely organized tribes, but a nation under God. In fact, the month in which the Israelites left Egypt, originally called Aviv but subsequently renamed Nisan, was designated as the first month of the year (Exodus 12:2), thus signifying its extreme importance.

The underlying thought of freedom for all people is the guiding principle for the celebration of this festival. So important and historic has been the attainment of our freedom in the life of the Jewish people that the phrase "remembering the Exodus from Egypt" appears frequently in our prayers, including the blessing over the wine.

CALENDAR

Pesach falls on the fourteenth of the Hebrew month of Nisan, which is usually in April or sometimes May. The Jewish sign of the zodiac for Nisan is a lamb, which is intended to remind us of the lamb used for the Pesach sacrifice in Temple times.

The story of Pesach begins many centuries ago when God commanded Moses to go to Egypt and ask King Pharaoh to let the Israelites go. Pharaoh was not afraid of Moses and would not let the people go. After Moses and his brother Aaron left the palace, terrible things began to happen to the Egyptians. First the water turned to blood. Then followed grasshoppers, swarming insects, frogs, hail, and even darkness. The last of the ten plagues was the worst of all. Every firstborn Egyptian male child died, but the angel of God passed over the homes of the Israelites. Finally, Pharaoh agreed to let the Israelites leave Egypt. Because they left in haste, their bread did not have time to rise. Matzah is eaten today at the Pesach family dinner, called a Seder, to commemorate the unleavened bread of the Israelites when they departed from Egypt.

After the Israelites left Egypt they traveled to the Sea of Reeds, or the Red Sea. But Pharaoh changed his mind and wanted the Israelites to remain his slaves. So he led his soldiers after them. When the Israelites arrived at the Red Sea, a great miracle occurred, and the sea parted. The Israelites crossed on the dry land, but when the Egyptians tried to follow, the waters closed in again. The children of Israel were safe on the shore, and Pharaoh and his army drowned in the sea. The Pesach Seder is a reenactment of this amazing story of freedom. Traditionally, it is held on both the first and the second night of Pesach.

CELEBRATIONS

In the Synagogue

On the day before Pesach, we observe the custom of the fast of the firstborn. This is in commemoration of the miraculous deliverance of the firstborn Israelites in Egypt. The rabbis, wishing to spare the firstborn the affliction of fasting, ingeniously suggested that they partake of a se'udat mitzvah—a religious obligatory meal. This is customarily done by celebrating in the synagogue, immediately after the morning service on the eve of Pesach, a siyyum, the conclusion of a talmudic tractate. Since an event of this kind is a festive occasion involving a meal, the participants are exempted from fasting.

The synagogue services during the week of Pesach are a bit longer than usual, due to additional prayers and Torah readings. The Hallel psalms of praise are chanted. The Torah reading for the first day deals with the institution of the festival in Egypt, the slaying of the firstborn, and Israel's departure from Egypt (Exodus 12:21–51). It is followed by a reading from a second Torah scroll, dealing with the ordinances concerning the special festival sacrifices in the Temple (Numbers 28:16–25). The Haftarah (from the Book of Joshua) describes the crossing of the Israelites into the Promised Land, where they celebrate Pesach for the first time in their own country. In the Musaf additional service, a special prayer for dew in Israel is recited.

Beginning on the second night of Pesach, the religious obligation of counting the *omer* is performed. The *omer* was an offering of barley that was brought to the ancient Temple on the eve of the second day of Pesach. The period between Pesach and Shavuot is referred to as the Omer. By counting the days of this period for seven weeks, we heighten our anticipation of the celebration of the festival of Shavuot, which commemorates the receiving of the Torah on Mount Sinai.

On the second day of Pesach a pattern similar to that of the first follows. The Hallel psalms of praise are chanted, and in the Torah reading we hear of the institution of the festivals (Leviticus 22:26–23:44). The Haftarah (from the book of Second Kings) tells of King Josiah's cleansing of the Temple and its restoration to the worship of God.

The third through the sixth days of Pesach are called the intermediate days, or Chol Hamo'eid. The Hallel service is abbreviated, revealing the compassionate nature of the Jewish people. We shorten our singing of prayers of praise out of pity for the Egyptians who suffered so much during this period.

The Sabbath of Chol Hamo'eid presents a Torah reading that speaks of God's Thirteen Attributes of mercy. It concludes with a brief review of the festivals (Exodus 33:12–34:26). The Haftarah (from the Book of Ezekiel) describes the prophet Ezekiel's famous vision of the Valley of the Dry Bones, symbolizing Israel's future rebirth as a nation. It is also customary on this Sabbath to read the Song of Songs, an allegorical love story in which "the beloved" is taken to be God and "the bride" is the people of Israel. The reading of the book marks the beginning of the courtship of Israel and God, before, metaphorically speaking, they are finally wedded at Mount Sinai by Israel's acceptance of the Torah. Another reason given for the reading of the Song of Songs is that it is a song of spring and renewal.

The seventh day of Pesach was the time when the Egyptians were drowned in the Red Sea. The Torah reading that morning is the beautiful hymn of thanksgiving sung by the Israelites after they safely crossed the sea (Exodus 13:17-15:26). The Haftarah is a song of thanksgiving by David, the second king of Israel. In it David praises God for giving him victory over his enemies.

The eighth day of Pesach (not observed by many Reform and Reconstructionist Jews) presents a Torah reading that speaks of the laws of the three Pilgrim Festivals—Sukkot, Pesach, and Shavuot (Deuteronomy 15:19–16:17). The Haftarah (from the Book of Isaiah) contains the great vision of the Messianic era when peace and harmony will reign supreme among people and animals, a time when the "wolf will dwell with the lamb and the leopard will lie down with the kid."

In the Home
On the day before Pesach, thorough preparations are made to remove the *chametz*, generally defined as the leavened product that results when the grains of wheat, rye, barley, oats, or spelt come into contact with water for more than a minimum of eighteen minutes. Thus, foods made from these grains are prohibited during Pesach. In addition, Ashkenazic Jews do not eat rice, corn, peas, and peanuts, or any derivatives thereof. Flour could be ground from these vegetables and

the breads baked from them would look like breads of pure chametz, which might be confusing to people. Sephardic Jews, on the other hand, have always served many wonderful side dishes made of rice and corn.

Cleaning for Pesach is the most thorough spring cleaning imaginable. Floors are vacuumed and shelves scrubbed. The entire family is usually involved in this meticulous cleaning. In many communities the rabbi buys the chametz from the people and sells it collectively to a non-Jew. This guarantees that no chametz will be in the possession of the households.

The Talmud (Pesachim 1:1) rules that we must search for the chametz using the light of a flame. As night falls on the thirteenth of Nisan, the family searches for the chametz, using a candle, a feather which acts as a broom, and a wooden spoon into which the pieces of bread are scooped. A blessing is recited before beginning the actual search. The next morning the chametz is burned, often at a small bonfire at the synagogue.

That evening is the first of two Seder meals, the highlight of the festival of Pesach. The Seder is more than simply a meal. It is a complete service that uses a storybook called a Haggadah and special foods and rituals that reenact the exodus of the Jewish people from Egypt. Among the objects on the table during the Seder service are matzah, wine, salt water (symbolizing the Israelites' tears), and a Seder plate. On the plate there are the following: bitter herbs, called *maror* in Hebrew (symbolizing the bitterness of slavery), a roasted egg (symbolizing the festival offering), a roasted shankbone (symbolizing the Pesach offering), a green vegetable called *karpas* in Hebrew (symbolizing spring), and *charoset*, a mixture of chopped apples and nuts, wine and spices, symbolizing the mortar used to build the Egyptian pyramids.

The Seder program consists of fourteen different ceremonies:

1. *Kadeish*   Blessing over wine
2. *Ur'chatz*   Washing hands without a blessing
3. *Karpas*   Eating green things
4. *Yachatz*   Breaking the middle matzah
5. *Magid*   Telling of the story
6. *Rachtzah*   Washing hands with a blessing
7. *Motzi matzah*   Blessing and eating of the matzah
8. *Maror*   Blessing and eating bitter herbs
9. *Koreikh*   Eating a sandwich of bitter herbs and charoset
10. *Shulchan oreikh* Serving of the festive meal
11. *Tzafun*   Finding the hidden afikoman
12. *Bareikh*   Reciting the blessing after the meal
13. *Hallel*   Singing psalms of praise
14. *Nirtzah*   Acceptance

BASIC BLESSINGS

Searching for Chametz

בָּרוּךְ אַתָּה יהוה אֱלֹהֵינוּ מֶלֶךְ הָעוֹלָם, אֲשֶׁר קִדְּשָׁנוּ בְּמִצְוֹתָיו וְצִוָּנוּ עַל בִּעוּר־חָמֵץ:

Barukh atah adonai eloheinu melekh ha'olam asher kid'shanu b'mitzvotav v'tzivanu al be'ur chametz.

Praised are You, Adonai our God, Sovereign of the Universe, who has made us holy by mitzvot and instructed us concerning the burning of the chametz.

After the Leaven Has Been Gathered

כָּל־חֲמִירָא וַחֲמִיעָא, דְּאִכָּא בִּרְשׁוּתִי, דַּחֲמִיתֵּהּ וּדְלָא חֲמִיתֵּהּ,
דִּבְעַרְתֵּהּ וּדְלָא בְעַרְתֵּהּ, לִבְטֵל וְלֶהֱוֵי הֶפְקֵר, כְּעַפְרָא דְאַרְעָא:

*Kol chamira vachami'a de'ika bir'shuti dachamiteih ud'la
chamiteih d'vi'arteh ud'la vi'arteih lib'teil v'lehevei hefker
d'ara.*

Any leaven that may still be in the house, which I have
not seen or have not removed, shall be as if it does not
exist, and as the dust of the earth.

Here are the blessings for the various parts of the Seder.

Kadeish

בָּרוּךְ אַתָּה יהוה אֱלֹהֵינוּ מֶלֶךְ הָעוֹלָם, בּוֹרֵא פְּרִי הַגָּפֶן
בָּרוּךְ אַתָּה יהוה אֱלֹהֵינוּ מֶלֶךְ הָעוֹלָם, אֲשֶׁר בָּחַר בָּנוּ מִכָּל־עָם
וְרוֹמְמָנוּ מִכָּל־לָשׁוֹן, וְקִדְּשָׁנוּ בְּמִצְוֹתָיו. וַתִּתֶּן לָנוּ יהוה אֱלֹהֵינוּ
בְּאַהֲבָה (שַׁבָּתוֹת לִמְנוּחָה וּ)מוֹעֲדִים לְשִׂמְחָה, חַגִּים וּזְמַנִּים לְשָׂשׂוֹן,
אֶת־יוֹם (הַשַּׁבָּת הַזֶּה וְאֶת־יוֹם) חַג הַמַּצּוֹת הַזֶּה, זְמַן חֵרוּתֵנוּ,
(בְּאַהֲבָה) מִקְרָא קֹדֶשׁ, זֵכֶר לִיצִיאַת מִצְרָיִם. כִּי־בָנוּ בָחַרְתָּ וְאוֹתָנוּ
קִדַּשְׁתָּ מִכָּל־הָעַמִּים, (וְשַׁבָּת) וּמוֹעֲדֵי קָדְשֶׁךָ (בְּאַהֲבָה וּבְרָצוֹן)
בְּשִׂמְחָה וּבְשָׂשׂוֹן הִנְחַלְתָּנוּ. בָּרוּךְ אַתָּה יְיָ, מְקַדֵּשׁ (הַשַּׁבָּת וְ)
יִשְׂרָאֵל וְהַזְּמַנִּים.

*Barukh atah adonai eloheinu melekh ha'olam, borei p'ri
hagafen. Barukh atah adonai eloheinu melekh ha'olam,
asher bachar banu mikol am v'rom'manu mikol lashon
v'kid'shanu b'mitzvotav vatiten lanu adonai eloheinu b'ahavah (shabbatot limenuchah u) mo'adim l'simchah chagim
uz'manim l'sasson et yom (hashabbat hazeh v'et yom)
chag hamatzot hazeh, z'man cheiruteinu (b'ahavah) mikra
kodesh zeikher litzi'at mitzrayim. Ki vanu vacharta v'otanu*

kidashta mikol ha'amim (v'shabbat) umo'adei kodsh'kha (b'ahavah uv'ratzon) b'simchah uv'sasson hinchaltanu. Barukh atah adonai, m'kadesh (hashabbat v') yisra'eil v'haz'manim.

Praised are You, Eternal our God, Sovereign of the Universe who creates fruit of the vine.

Praised are You, Eternal our God, Sovereign of the Universe who has chosen and distinguished us from among all others by adding holiness to our lives with mitzvot. Lovingly have You given us (Shabbat for rest,) festivals for joy and holidays for happiness, among them this (Shabbat and this) day of Pesach, season of our liberation, a day of sacred assembly recalling the Exodus from Egypt. Thus You have chosen us, endowing us with holiness from among all peoples by granting us (Shabbat and) Your hallowed festivals (lovingly and gladly) in happiness and joy. Praised are You, God who hallows (Shabbat and) the people Israel and the festivals.

בָּרוּךְ אַתָּה יהוה אֱלֹהֵינוּ מֶלֶךְ הָעוֹלָם, שֶׁהֶחֱיָנוּ וְקִיְּמָנוּ וְהִגִּיעָנוּ לַזְּמַן הַזֶּה.

Barukh atah adonai eloheinu melekh ha'olam sheheche-yanu v'kiymanu v'higi'anu laz'man hazeh.

Praised are You, Adonai our God, Sovereign of the Universe, who has kept us alive, sustained us, and helped us to reach this moment.

Karpas

בָּרוּךְ אַתָּה יהוה אֱלֹהֵינוּ מֶלֶךְ הָעוֹלָם, בּוֹרֵא פְּרִי הָאֲדָמָה:

*Barukh atah adonai eloheinu melekh ha'olam borei p'ri
ha'adamah.*

Praised are You, Adonai our God, Sovereign of the
Universe, who creates the fruit of the earth.

Rachtzah

בָּרוּךְ אַתָּה יהוה אֱלֹהֵינוּ מֶלֶךְ הָעוֹלָם, אֲשֶׁר קִדְּשָׁנוּ בְּמִצְוֹתָיו
וְצִוָּנוּ עַל נְטִילַת יָדָיִם.

*Barukh atah adonai eloheinu melekh ha'olam asher
kid'shanu b'mitzvotav v'tzivanu al n'tilat yadayim.*

Praised are You, Adonai our God, Sovereign of the
Universe, who has made us holy by mitzvot and instructed
us concerning the washing of our hands.

Motzi Matzah

בָּרוּךְ אַתָּה יהוה אֱלֹהֵינוּ מֶלֶךְ הָעוֹלָם, הַמּוֹצִיא לֶחֶם מִן הָאָרֶץ.

*Barukh atah adonai eloheinu melekh ha'olam hamotzi
lechem min ha'aretz.*

Praised are You, Adonai our God, Sovereign of the
Universe, who brings forth bread from the earth.

בָּרוּךְ אַתָּה יהוה אֱלֹהֵינוּ מֶלֶךְ הָעוֹלָם, אֲשֶׁר קִדְּשָׁנוּ בְּמִצְוֹתָיו
וְצִוָּנוּ עַל אֲכִילַת מַצָּה:

*Barukh atah adonai eloheinu melekh ha'olam asher
kid'shanu b'mitzvotav v'tzivanu al achilat matzah.*

Praised are You, Adonai our God, Sovereign of the Universe, who has made us holy by mitzvot and instructed us concerning the eating of unleavened bread.

Maror

בָּרוּךְ אַתָּה יהוה אֱלֹהֵינוּ מֶלֶךְ הָעוֹלָם, אֲשֶׁר קִדְּשָׁנוּ בְּמִצְוֹתָיו וְצִוָּנוּ עַל אֲכִילַת מָרוֹר:

Barukh atah adonai eloheinu melekh ha'olam asher kid'shanu b'mitzvotav v'tzivanu al achilat maror.

Praised are You, Adonai our God, Sovereign of the Universe, who has made us holy by mitzvot and instructed us concerning the eating of bitter herbs.

Bareikh

רַבּוֹתַי נְבָרֵךְ.

Rabotai n'vareikh

Friends, let us give thanks.

The others respond, and the leader repeats:

יְהִי שֵׁם יְיָ מְבֹרָךְ מֵעַתָּה וְעַד עוֹלָם.

Y'hi sheim adonai m'vorakh mei'atah v'ad olam.

May God be praised now and forever.

The leader continues:

בִּרְשׁוּת רַבּוֹתַי, נְבָרֵךְ (אֱלֹהֵינוּ) שֶׁאָכַלְנוּ מִשֶּׁלוֹ.

Bir'shut rabotai n'vareikh (eloheinu) she'akhalnu mishelo.

With your consent friends, let us praise (our God) the
One of whose food we have partaken.

The others respond, and the leader repeats:

בָּרוּךְ (אֱלֹהֵינוּ) שֶׁאָכַלְנוּ מִשֶּׁלוֹ וּבטוּבוֹ חָיִינוּ.

Barukh (eloheinu) she'akhalnu mishelo uv'tuvo chayinu.

Praised be (our God) the One whose food we have partaken and by whose goodness we live.

Leader and others:

בָּרוּךְ הוּא וּבָרוּךְ שְׁמוֹ.

Barukh hu uvarukh sh'mo.

Praised be God and praised be God's name.

בָּרוּךְ אַתָּה יהוה אֱלֹהֵינוּ מֶלֶךְ הָעוֹלָם,הַזָּן אֶת־הָעוֹלָם כֻּלּוֹ בְּטוּבוֹ,
בְּחֵן בְּחֶסֶד וּבְרַחֲמִים. הוּא נוֹתֵן לֶחֶם לְכָל־בָּשָׂר כִּי לְעוֹלָם חַסְדּוֹ.
וּבְטוּבוֹ הַגָּדוֹל תָּמִיד לֹא חָסַר לָנוּ וְאַל יֶחְסַר לָנוּ מָזוֹן לְעוֹלָם
וָעֶד בַּעֲבוּר שְׁמוֹ הַגָּדוֹל, כִּי הוּא אֵל זָן וּמְפַרְנֵס לַכֹּל וּמֵטִיב לַכֹּל
וּמֵכִין מָזוֹן לְכָל־בְּרִיּוֹתָיו אֲשֶׁר בָּרָא. בָּרוּךְ אַתָּה יהוה, הַזָּן אֶת־הַכֹּל.

Barukh atah adonai, eloheinu melekh ha'olam, hazan et
ha'olam kulo b'tuvo b'chein, b'chesed, uv'rachamim. Hu
notein lechem l'khol basar, ki l'olam chasdo. Uv'tuvo hagadol, tamid lo chasar lanu, v'al yechsar lanu mazon l'olam

*va'ed ba'avur sh'mo hagadol, ki hu el zan um'farneis lakol,
umeitiv lakol, umeikhin mazon l'khol b'riyotav asher bara.
Barukh atah adonai, hazan et hakol.*

Praised are You, Eternal, our God, Sovereign of the Universe who sustains the whole world with kindness and
compassion. You provide food for every creature, for
Your love endures forever. Your great goodness has never
failed us. Your great glory assures us nourishment. All life
is God's creation and God is good to all, providing every
creature with food and sustenance. Praised are You, God
who sustains all life.

נוֹדֶה לְךָ יְיָ אֱלֹהֵינוּ עַל שֶׁהִנְחַלְתָּ לַאֲבוֹתֵינוּ אֶרֶץ חֶמְדָּה טוֹבָה
וּרְחָבָה, בְּרִית וְתוֹרָה, חַיִּים וּמָזוֹן. יִתְבָּרַךְ שִׁמְךָ בְּפִי כָל-חַי תָּמִיד
לְעוֹלָם וָעֶד, כַּכָּתוּב: וְאָכַלְתָּ וְשָׂבַעְתָּ וּבֵרַכְתָּ אֶת-יְיָ אֱלֹהֶיךָ עַל
הָאָרֶץ הַטּוֹבָה אֲשֶׁר נָתַן לָךְ. בָּרוּךְ אַתָּה יְיָ, עַל הָאָרֶץ וְעַל
הַמָּזוֹן.

*Nodeh l'kha adonai eloheinu al shehinchalta la'avoteinu
eretz chemdah, tovah ur'chavah, b'rit v'torah, chayim um-
azon. Yitbarakh shimkha bfi khol chai tamid l'olam va'ed.
Kakatuv v'akhalta v'savata uveirakhta et adonai elohekha
al ha'aretz hatovah asher natan lakh. Barukh atah adonai,
al ha'aretz v'al hamazon.*

We thank you, God, for the pleasing, ample, desirable
land which You gave to our ancestors, for the covenant
and Torah, for life and sustenance. May You forever be
praised by all who live, as it is written in the Torah:
"When you have eaten and are satisfied, you shall praise
the Eternal your God for the good land which He has
given you." Praised are You, God, for the land and for
sustenance.

וּבְנֵה יְרוּשָׁלַיִם עִיר הַקֹדֶשׁ בִּמְהֵרָה בְּיָמֵינוּ. בָּרוּךְ אַתָּה יְיָ, בּוֹנֵה בְּרַחֲמָיו יְרוּשָׁלַיִם. אָמֵן.

Uv'neih yerushalayim ir hakodesh bimheirah v'yameinu. Barukh atah adonai, boneh v'rachamav yerushalayim. Amen.

Fully rebuild Jerusalem, the holy city, soon in our time. Praised are You, Lord, who in mercy rebuilds Jerusalem. Amen.

בָּרוּךְ אַתָּה יהוה אֱלֹהֵינוּ מֶלֶךְ הָעוֹלָם, הַמֶּלֶךְ הַטּוֹב וְהַמֵּטִיב לַכֹּל. הוּא הֵטִיב, הוּא מֵטִיב, הוּא יֵיטִיב לָנוּ. הוּא גְמָלָנוּ הוּא גוֹמְלֵנוּ הוּא יִגְמְלֵנוּ לָעַד חֵן וָחֶסֶד וְרַחֲמִים וִיזַכֵּנוּ לִימוֹת הַמָּשִׁיחַ.

Barukh atah adonai, eloheinu melekh ha'olam, hamelekh hatov v'hameitiv lakol. Hu heitiv, hu meitiv, hu yeitiv lanu. Hu g'malanu, hu gomleinu, hu yigm'leinu la'ad chein vachesed v'rachamim, vizakeinu limot hamashi'ach.

Praised are You, God, Sovereign of the Universe who is good to all, whose goodness is constant through all time. Favor us with kindness and compassion now and in the future as in the past. May we be worthy of the days of the Messiah.

[On Shabbat add:

הָרַחֲמָן, הוּא יַנְחִילֵנוּ יוֹם שֶׁכֻּלוֹ שַׁבָּת וּמְנוּחָה לְחַיֵּי הָעוֹלָמִים.

Harachaman hu yanchileinu yom shekulo shabbat umenu-chah l'chayei ha'olamim.

May the Merciful grant us a day of true shabbat rest, reflecting the life of eternity.]

[On festivals:

הָרַחֲמָן, הוּא יַנְחִילֵנוּ יוֹם שֶׁכֻּלוֹ טוֹב.

Harachaman hu yanchileinu yom shekulo tov.

May the Merciful grant us a day filled with the spirit of the festival.]

וְנִשָּׂא בְרָכָה מֵאֵת יְיָ וּצְדָקָה מֵאֱלֹהֵי יִשְׁעֵנוּ וְנִמְצָא חֵן וְשֵׂכֶל טוֹב בְּעֵינֵי אֱלֹהִים וְאָדָם. עֹשֶׂה שָׁלוֹם בִּמְרוֹמָיו הוּא יַעֲשֶׂה שָׁלוֹם עָלֵינוּ וְעַל כָּל-יִשְׂרָאֵל, וְאִמְרוּ אָמֵן.

V'nisa v'rakhah mei'eit adonai utz'dakah mei'elohei yish'einu. V'nimtza chein v'seikhel tov b'einei elohim v'adam. Oseh shalom bimromav hu ya'aseh shalom aleinu v'al kol yisra'eil. V'imru amen.

May we receive blessings from God, loving-kindness from the God of our deliverance. May we find grace and good favor before God and all people. May God who brings peace to the universe bring peace to us and to all the people Israel. And let us say: Amen.

MAKING FAMILY

1. Make several different kinds of charoset representing different countries around the world. Here are several recipes to get you started.

Moroccan Charoset

1 cup chopped dates, chopped walnuts, and sweet red wine.

Yemenite Charoset

15 pitted chopped dates and dried figs, 1 teaspoon ground ginger, red wine, and 1 small chile pepper.

Israeli Charoset

> 2 peeled, cored, and grated apples,
> 2 mashed bananas,
> 14 chopped and pitted dates,
> ½ cup blanched chopped almonds,
> ¼ cup matzah meal,
> juice and rind of a half lemon,
> juice and rind of a half orange,
> ¼ cup sweet red wine,
> 1 teaspoon cinnamon and sugar.

Combine all of these ingredients, adding enough wine to make a paste.

2. Collect wheat money (*ma'ot chittim*) and give it to your favorite charity.

3. Donate your chametz to a non-Jewish food pantry for the hungry.

4. There are many innovative ideas that can enhance your Seder meal. Here are several for you to try. If you'd like more, you may want to refer to our own *Discovery Haggadah* (available from Ktav).

a. Leave a fifth cup at your Seder empty to symbolize oppressed people everywhere.

b. Carry the afikoman in a bag on your shoulder so that you can feel like the Israelites who hastily left Egypt.

c. Pretend that you are slaves and beat each other using green scallions. Share with each family member how you might have felt if you had been a slave in Egypt.

d. Use props during the reciting of the Ten Plagues (e.g., rubber frogs, red food coloring that will make water look like blood, etc.).

e. Have someone dress up as Elijah and invite him in to your Seder.

GLOSSARY

Afikoman. "Dessert." The hidden matzah eaten just before the Blessing After the Meal.
B'dikat Chametz. The ceremonial search for leaven on the night before Pesach.
Bi'ur Chametz. The ceremonial burning of the leaven on the morning of the eve of Pesach.
Chad Gadya. "The Only Kid." A favorite Pesach song.
Chag Hamatzot. "Feast of Unleavened Bread." Another name for the Pesach festival.
Chametz. Foods that are considered leaven and therefore forbidden on Pesach.
Charoset. Mixture of apples, cinammon, nuts, and wine, symbolizing the mortar used by the Israelite slaves.
Chol Hamo'eid. The intermediate days of the festival.
Counting of the Omer. Ceremonial counting of the weeks and days between Pesach and Shavuot.
Erev Pesach. The eve of Pesach.

Four Questions. The questions asked by the youngest children during the early part of the Seder.

Haggadah. The book used at the Pesach Seder.

Karpas. The green vegetable on the Seder plate, symbolizing spring and renewal.

Mah Nishtanah. Opening words of the Four Questions, meaning "why is it different?"

Ma'ot Chittim. Special fund to help the needy before Pesach.

Maror. Bitter herbs.

Matzah. Unleavened bread.

Omer. Measure of barley brought to the Temple during the weeks between Pesach and Shavuot.

Seder. Literally "Order." The Pesach dinner and reading of the Haggadah.

Shir Hashirim. Song of Songs. Biblical book read on the Intermediate Sabbath of Pesach.

Z'ro'ah. The roasted bone (or meat) on the Seder plate.

Lag B'omer

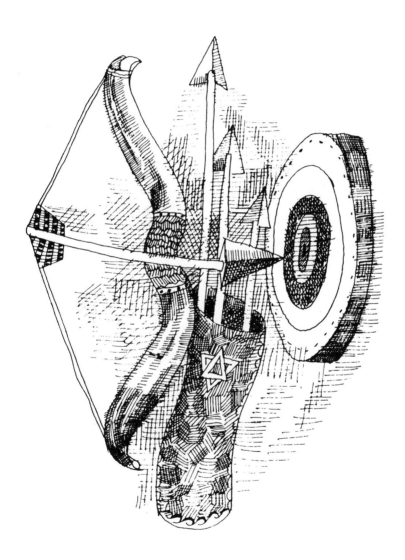

Lag B'omer

WORDS OF TORAH

The Book of Leviticus (23:15–16) tells us that we "shall count from the eve of the second day of Pesach, when an omer of grain is to be brought as an offering, seven complete weeks." By counting the days of this period, known in Hebrew as Sefirat Ha'omer ("counting of the omer"), we recall the events leading from the exodus from Egypt to the gift of the revelation of the Torah at Mount Sinai, commemorated by Shavuot. Lag B'omer is the thirty-third day of the counting. Unlike most Jewish festivals, it is not a religious holiday, it is not mentioned in the Bible, and there are no specific prayers associated with it. And yet there are certain customs that are observed on this very unique holiday, which commemorates the end of a plague that killed many of Rabbi Akiba's students.

BACK TO BASICS

In the course of the long centuries of exile, the days between Pesach and Shavuot have on many occasions been periods of distress and misfortune for the Jewish people. For example, in the Middle Ages, the Crusader massacre of the Jews of Jerusalem took place at this time. In Roman times, according to tradition, a great plague raged among the students of Rabbi Akiba during this period, coming to an end on the eighteenth of Iyar, which is Lag B'omer. Another tradition concerns Shimon bar Yochai, a distinguished disciple of Rabbi Akiba. Sentenced to death by the Romans for his participation in a revolt against them, he hid in a cave and did not come out until Lag B'omer, when he learned that the enemy had been defeated. Because of the connection to Rabbi Akiba and his students, Lag B'omer is known as the Scholars' Festival, and Jewish children throughout the world hold special celebrations to mark the occasion.

CALENDAR

Lag B'omer always falls on the eighteen of the month of Iyar, thirty-three days after the beginning of Pesach. To lend special emphasis to the importance of the spring barley harvest, the Israelites were instructed to bring the omer (the yield of a sheaf of barley) to the Temple priest, beginning on the second day of Pesach. On this day they were to begin to count forty-nine days until Shavuot, the festival of the wheat harvest.

The counting takes place at nightfall, since the reaping of the omer took place at night. The method of counting was always to mention both the days and the weeks. For example, "This day completes thirty-three days, which is four weeks and five days." The counting is preceded by the recitation of a special blessing.

CELEBRATIONS

In the Synagogue
Many synagogues hold picnics and outings on Lag B'omer, with food, music, dance, sporting events (often in the form of a competitive Maccabiah), and other festivities. It is often the last social get-together before the summer vacation. Jewish weddings are often held on Lag B'omer as well. Some synagogues hold a bonfire and cookout on Lag B'omer which often includes Israeli singing and dancing.

In Israel, Lag B'omer is a day for bonfire celebrations. The most famous is held at the village of Meron, near the northern city of Safed. Shimon bar Yochai is said to be buried there, and huge crowds gather at his tomb for this very happy celebration. It is said that while Rabbi Shimon bar Yochai was hiding in his cave he wrote a famous holy book of mysticism called the *Zohar*. On Lag B'omer, many of the Hasidim study portions of the *Zohar* during the special celebrations at Meron.

Finally, some synagogue schools have turned Lag B'omer into a day for honoring their religious-school teachers. Special assemblies and parties are held, and awards are often given to the teachers.

In the Home

The custom of children playing with bow and arrow on Lag B'omer is traced to the legend that the rainbow, a symbol of peace, did not appear during the lifetime of Shimon bar Yochai because of his saintliness. Others associate the custom with the tradition that the students of Rabbi Akiba deceived the Romans by carrying bows and arrows to pretend that they were hunting when in fact they were studying Torah, which the Romans had forbidden.

Since the days preceding Lag B'omer were traditionally considered days of mourning, and therefore haircutting and shaving were not permitted, Lag B'omer became a time for youngsters to be given their first haircut. Often their parents plied them with wine and sweets to celebrate this happy event.

Some families use Lag B'omer as the occasion for a family outing or picnic.

BASIC BLESSINGS

Prayer for Counting the Omer on Lag B'omer

בָּרוּךְ אַתָּה יהוה אֱלֹהֵינוּ מֶלֶךְ הָעוֹלָם, אֲשֶׁר קִדְּשָׁנוּ בְּמִצְוֹתָיו
וְצִוָּנוּ עַל סְפִרַת הָעֹמֶר.
הַיּוֹם שְׁלֹשָׁה וּשְׁלֹשִׁים יוֹם שֶׁהֵם אַרְבָּעָה שָׁבוּעוֹת וַחֲמִשָּׁה יָמִים
לָעֹמֶר:

*Barukh atah adonai eloheinu melekh ha'olam asher
kid'shanu b'mitzvotav v'tzivanu al s'firat ha'omer.
Hayom sh'loshah ush'loshim yom shehem arba'ah shavu'ot
v'chamisha yamim la'omer.*

Praised are You, Adonai our God, Sovereign of the
Universe, who has made us holy by mitzvot and who
instructed us to count the omer. Today is the thirty-third
day of the omer.

MAKING FAMILY

1. Go on a picnic or family outing with your own family or
   have several families join you.

2. Get together with several families and make a campfire
   which includes good eating and singing.

3. Each night, before the counting of the omer, take a
   nonperishable grain product and place it in a box. When
   the last night of the omer has been counted, take all of
   the grain products to a local food pantry as your way of
   helping the hungry.

4. Make a donation to Mazon: A Jewish Response to Hunger,
   as a family on Lag B'omer.

GLOSSARY

Akiba. The famous rabbi and scholar who urged the Jewish people to rebel against the Romans.

Bow and arrows. Symbols connected with Lag B'omer

Lag. The Hebrew letters with the alpha-numerical value of 33.

Omer. A measure of barley brought to the Temple between Pesach and Shavuot as a way of counting the days between these two festivals.

Scholars' Day. Another name for Lag B'omer.

Yom Ha'atzma'ut

Yom Ha'atzma'ut

WORDS OF TORAH

For the Jew, Israel is the center of the world. The longing for Israel, and still more for Jerusalem, that we have felt throughout our history and our wanderings is best described by the Talmud's comments on the text "For your servants delight in her stones and love her dust." The rabbis of the Talmud illustrate the meaning of "delight" and "love" in this passage by telling us that Rav Abba used to kiss the stones of Akko, Rabbi Chanina would mend Israel's roads, and Rav Chiyya bar Gamla would roll in the dust of the Holy Land (Ketubot 112a–b).

BACK TO BASICS

In 1897, Theodor Herzl, known as the father of modern Zionism, convened the First Zionist Congress in Basel, Switzerland. At that time the Turks ruled Palestine, only to be replaced by the British following World War I. In the 1930s, amid Arab pressure, the British issued several White Papers which limited immigration to Israel. The Jewish community responded with a flood of illegal immigration known as Aliyah Bet. Eventually, in the shadow of the Holocaust, the Jewish people refused to accept the rule of other nations any longer. We had been without a home for nearly 2,000 years.

Yom Ha'atzma'ut marks the rebirth of the modern state of Israel, the Third Commonwealth of the Jewish people.

Since this is a relatively new occasion on the Jewish calendar, its observance is still very fluid. Unlike other holidays and festivals, where the ceremonies have developed over time, there is still a great deal of discussion concerning the proper way to observe Israel's independence as a modern nation.

Israel Independence Day is preceded by Yom Hazikaron (Remembrance Day) for all those who have fallen in defense of Israel's independence and security. On that day, special prayers are said, cemeteries are visited, and memorial ceremonies take place. In the middle of the day, a two-minute silence is observed.

Israel is constantly in our thoughts. Thus we say each day, as part of the Blessing After the Meal, "And rebuild Jerusalem, the holy city, speedily, and in our day. Praised are You, God, who rebuilds Jerusalem."

CALENDAR

Israel Independence Day falls on Iyar 5 and corresponds to May 14, 1948 (5708), the day on which the Declaration of Independence was issued and the State of Israel established. The holiday itself was established by law in 1949. When this date falls on a Friday or Shabbat, it is celebrated on Thursday. Indirectly related to Yom Ha'atzma'ut is Yom Yerushalayim, the Day of Jerusalem, which takes place on 28 Iyar, the day in June 1967 when Jerusalem's Old City, including all of east Jerusalem (formerly in the hands of Jordan), was reunited with new (or west) Jerusalem during the Six-Day War.

CELEBRATIONS

In Israel, there is dancing in the streets, a fireworks display, and lots of picnics. Yom Ha'atzma'ut is inaugurated on the evening of the festival by a ceremony at Mount Herzl in Jerusalem on the site of the grave of Theodor Herzl. The speaker of the Knesset lights a torch from which twelve other torches are lit, one for each of the twelve tribes of ancient Israel. This ceremony is concluded by a gun salute, one round for each year of Israel's existence as a modern state. For the first twenty years, there were military parades. These have been replaced by a march of Gadna, Israel's Youth Corps. In Haifa, a dance parade is held, and there are official receptions throughout the country.

In the Synagogue

Following the Sephardi and Yemenite formula for Tisha B'av, the day is announced in some synagogues as follows: "Hear ye, our brethren . . . today . . . years have elapsed since the beginning of our redemption marked by the establishment of the State."

The evening service is introduced by Psalms 107, 97, and 98. The service is concluded by the blowing of the shofar and this prayer, "May it be Your will, that as we have been deemed worthy to witness the beginning of redemption, so also may we be deemed worthy to hear the shofar announcing the Messiah speedily in our days."

The morning services includes Sabbath and festival psalms, the Nishmat prayer, Hallel, and the Haftarah portion which is also read on the last day of Pesach (Isaiah 10:32–11:12), but without the accompanying benedictions. Tachanun is omitted.

There has been some controversy concerning the reading of Hallel and the Haftarah without benedictions (since this is not a holiday which is announced in the Torah). And an optional Torah portion has been added in some communities (Deuteronomy 7:1–8:18 or 30:1–10).

In the Home
The major stress has been after the manner of a Pesach Seder, and there are even some Haggadah-type volumes available.

MAKING FAMILY

Dining on Israeli foods is a good way to observe Yom Ha'atzma'ut. Here are a few recipes.

Falafel
This is a tasty treat sold on street corners and served at parties.

> 1½ pounds chickpeas (canned or fresh; if fresh, soak overnight)
> 6 cloves garlic
> 2 teaspoons salt
> 2 hot peppers
> 1 cup cold water
> flour
> cooking oil

Grind soaked (uncooked) peas with garlic and salt, using fine blade of a food chopper. Soak hot peppers in cold water for five minutes. Mix water and seeds of peppers (not skins!) with chickpeas. Rolling in hands covered with flour, form the mixture into small balls about the size of walnuts. Drop into boiling oil until balls turn golden brown in color. Serve wrapped in pita with green salad, pickles, and olives. Falafel is often served with hot sauce and techina.

Leben (Israeli yogurt)

>   1 cup milk
>   1 teaspoon sour cream

Boil the milk. Do not overboil. Let cool for 10 minutes. Add the sour cream and mix well. Cover the milk. Let it stand at room temperature for 24 hours. Refrigerate for 24 to 48 hours until ready to eat.

Pita Bread

>   1 cup sifted flour
>   ¾ cup water
>   pinch of salt

Mix all ingredients together until dough is smooth. Roll out on a floured board with a rolling pin. Use the bottom of a glass to indent the circles. Place on a slightly greased baking sheet and bake in a preheated oven at 400 degrees for 20 minutes, or until slightly golden in color. Remove from oven, and let cool for 10 to 15 minutes. Slice the pita at the top to form a "pocket" for stuffing. Ready to eat when almost completely cool.

Israeli dancing is also fun. Try the following basic Israeli folk dance steps.

Tcherkessia
Right foot steps forward, left backward, right backward, left forward. (Four walking steps.)

Half Tcherkessia
Right foot steps forward, left backward. (Two walking steps.)

Double Tcherkessia
Right foot crosses in front of left, left foot backward in place, right to right side, and reverse. (Six walking steps—six counts.)

Mayim
Right foot crosses in front of left, left steps to the left side; right crosses behind left and left steps to the left side. (Four walking steps but moving in a circle clockwise.)

Harmonica
Right foot crosses in front of left, left backward, right to right side and hop on right.

Yemenite
Step on right foot to right side (bend right knee); left crosses behind right (on toe); right crosses in front of left (straight knee); fourth count is a pause.

Debka
Jump in place twice, with feet together. On the first jump, the body, from the waist down, turns to the left (upper part faces the circle center). On second jump, face center again.
All of the preceding steps can be reversed. The rhythm is four counts to a measure. In some dances, the rhythm of the steps is changed.

Hora
Stand in a circle, holding hands. Right foot to left of left foot. Make a small skip. Left foot step in place. Right foot to right of left foot. Make a small skip. Left foot. Step in place.

Hora Steps to Mayim
Stand in a circle, holding hands. Right foot to left of left foot.
Make a small skip. Left foot step in place. Right foot to right
of left foot. Make a small skip. Left foot. Step in place.
Repeat four times. Lift hand, joined together in a circle, and
step to center of circle. Clap hands. Step back to beginning
of circle. Repeat twice. Skip in place on one foot, two times.
Cross right foot in front of left foot and clap hands, four
times. Cross left foot in front of right foot and clap hands,
four times. Repeat twice. Begin from the beginning.

BASIC BLESSINGS

While there are no specific blessings associated with Yom
Ha'atzma'ut, the singing of Hatikvah, Israel's national anthem,
and the recitation of Psalm 122 and other psalms of pilgrimage
is most appropriate.

Hatikvah
   Kol od baleivav p'nimah   כָּל עוֹד בַּלֵּבָב פְּנִימָה
   Nefesh yehudi homiyah   נֶפֶשׁ יְהוּדִי הוֹמִיָּה
   Ul'fa'atei mizrach kadimah   וּלְפַאֲתֵי מִזְרָח קָדִימָה
   Ayin l'tziyon tzofiyah   עַיִן לְצִיּוֹן צוֹפִיָּה.

   Od lo avdah tikvatenu   עוֹד לֹא אָבְדָה תִקְוָתֵנוּ
   Hatikvah shenot alpayim   הַתִּקְוָה שְׁנוֹת אַלְפַּיִם
   Lih'yot am chofshi b'artzeinu   לִהְיוֹת עַם חָפְשִׁי בְּאַרְצֵנוּ
   Eretz tziyon virushalayim   בְּאֶרֶץ צִיּוֹן וִירוּשָׁלָיִם.

As long as deep in the heart
The soul of a Jew yearns,
And towards the East
An eye looks to Zion,

Our hope is not yet lost,
The hope of two thousand years,
To be a free people in our land,
The land of Zion and Jerusalem.

Psalm 122
Our feet are standing at your gates, Jerusalem. Jerusalem,
built as a city bound firmly together, where tribes once went
up to give thanks unto Adonai, where thrones of justice
were once set, thrones of the house of David. Pray for the
peace of Jerusalem; may those who love her prosper. May
peace be in her walls, tranquility in her towers. May Adonai
bless us from Zion and let us see the good of Jerusalem. Let
us see our children's children and peace upon Israel.

Adapted for use from Psalm 122
(Hebrew Union College–Jewish Institute of Religion,
Jerusalem)

GLOSSARY

Atzma'ut. Independence.
Hatikvah. "The Hope." Israel's national anthem.
Kumsitz. A kind of social gathering in which people come
    and sit.

Yom Hasho'ah

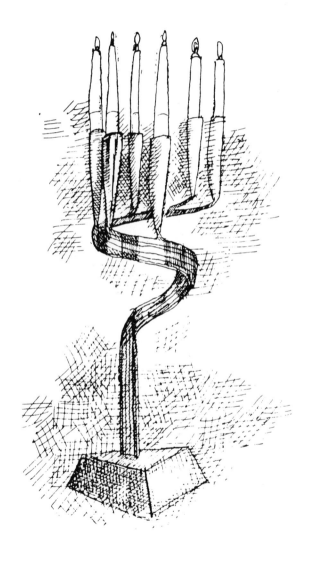

Yom Hasho'ah

WORDS OF TORAH

Ani ma'amin be'emunah sh'leimah. "I believe with perfect faith in the coming of the Messiah. And although the Messiah may tarry, nonetheless, I still believe." These words of prayerful hope and faith, adapted from one of the Thirteen Principles of Faith of the medieval philosopher Moses Maimonides, were spoken by the victims of the Holocaust even as they were led to their deaths.

BACK TO BASICS

In 1933, Adolf Hitler came to power in Germany. By the end of World War II (1945), he had destroyed six million Jews (and three million non-Jews) as part of his "Final Solution" to ethnically cleanse Germany and the lands he took by force and make them free of Jews.

Yom Hashoah is a reminder that as Jews we must all think of ourselves as having lost family during the Holocaust, just as we imagine ourselves as having been slaves in Egypt during our observance of Pesach.

CALENDAR

A resolution of the Knesset, Israel's national legislature, on April 12, 1951 designated the twenty-seventh of Nisan as "Holocaust and Ghetto Uprising Day, a day of perpetual remembrance for the House of Israel." Outside Israel, in the early years of the observance, it was customary to memorialize the Holocaust on April 19th, the day on which the Warsaw Ghetto Uprising began. The tenth of Tevet was established by the Israeli Chief Rabbinate as the day of Yahrzeit for Kaddish to be said by relatives of those who had lost family in the Holocaust.

OBSERVANCES

In Israel places of entertainment are closed on the eve of Yom Hashoah. Outside Israel observances differ from city to city. Some are interfaith. Like other observances which have become part of the Jewish calendar in the modern era, it will take several generations to fix the observance of Yom Hashoah.

In the Synagogue

Observances are generally held in combination with the evening worship service. Candles are lit and special prayers like El Malei Rachamim and Kaddish are added. Holocaust poems and literature are also added, as is the public testimony of survivors. Songs of the partisans are sung (in Yiddish, the Jewish folk language that was nearly destroyed in the Holocaust along with the people who spoke it). Sometimes Holocaust films are shown. And the Ani Ma'amin prayer is sung in the dirge-like melody that was sung by the victims of the Holocaust.

In the Home

Memorial candles are lit. Some people light one; others light six to acknowledge the six million Jews who perished.

MAKING FAMILY

While it is inappropriate to speak of family celebration in this context, it is most appropriate to talk about honoring family. In keeping with the biblical instruction for Pesach, "In every generation one is obligated to look on oneself as if personally delivered from Egypt," we extend this instruction to the remainder of Jewish history and to Yom Hashoah and the Holocaust. Whether or not we lost relatives in the Holocaust, we *all* lost family. It is important to remember them and to honor their memory by affirming and living the values of family.

You know that relative that you haven't spoken to in a long time because you were angry about some silly thing (that you may not even be able to remember). Call her now. Go visit him today. Drop them a note in order to make amends. And remember to discuss what you are doing with your kids. They will remember!

BASIC BLESSINGS

While there is no special blessing to be said as one lights the memorial candle, perhaps it is more appropriate to focus one's thoughts on the memory of those who perished in the Holocaust, many of whom were directly related to us. In addition, we say Kaddish for those from our family who perished and for those for whom there is no one to say Kaddish.

Kaddish

יִתְגַּדַּל וְיִתְקַדַּשׁ שְׁמֵהּ רַבָּא בְּעָלְמָא דִּי־בְרָא כִרְעוּתֵהּ, וְיַמְלִיךְ מַלְכוּתֵהּ בְּחַיֵּיכוֹן וּבְיוֹמֵיכוֹן וּבְחַיֵּי דְכָל־בֵּית יִשְׂרָאֵל, בַּעֲגָלָא וּבִזְמַן קָרִיב, וְאִמְרוּ: אָמֵן.

יְהֵא שְׁמֵהּ רַבָּא מְבָרַךְ לְעָלַם וּלְעָלְמֵי עָלְמַיָּא.
יִתְבָּרַךְ וְיִשְׁתַּבַּח, וְיִתְפָּאַר וְיִתְרוֹמַם וְיִתְנַשֵּׂא, וְיִתְהַדָּר וְיִתְעַלֶּה
וְיִתְהַלָּל שְׁמֵהּ דְּקוּדְשָׁא, בְּרִיךְ הוּא, לְעֵלָּא מִן־כָּל־בִּרְכָתָא וְשִׁירָתָא,
תֻּשְׁבְּחָתָא וְנֶחֱמָתָא דַּאֲמִירָן בְּעָלְמָא, וְאִמְרוּ: אָמֵן.
יְהֵא שְׁלָמָא רַבָּא מִן־שְׁמַיָּא וְחַיִּים עָלֵינוּ וְעַל־כָּל־יִשְׂרָאֵל, וְאִמְרוּ:
אָמֵן.
עֹשֶׂה שָׁלוֹם בִּמְרוֹמָיו, הוּא יַעֲשֶׂה שָׁלוֹם עָלֵינוּ וְעַל־כָּל־יִשְׂרָאֵל
וְאִמְרוּ: אָמֵן.

Yitgadal v'yitkadash sh'meih raba b'alma div'ra khir'uteih,
v'yamlikh malkhuteh b'chayekhon uv'yomeikhon uv'chayei
d'khol beit yisra'eil ba'agala uvizman kariv, v'imru amen.
Y'hei sh'meih raba m'varakh l'alam ul'almei almaya.
Yitbarakh v'yishtabach, v'yitpa'ar v'yitromam v'yitnasei,
v'yit-hadar v'yit'ale v'yit-halal sh'meih d'kudsha, b'rikh hu,
l'eila min kol birkhata v'shirata, tushb'chata v'nechemata,
da'amiran b'alma, v'imru: amen.
Y'hei sh'lama raba min sh'maya v'chayim aleinu v'al kol
yisra'eil, v'imru: amen.
Oseh Shalom bimromav, hu ya'aseh shalom aleinu v'al
kol yisra'eil, v'imru: amen.

Let the glory of God be extolled, let God's great name be
hallowed, in the world whose creation God willed. May
God's sovereignty soon prevail, in our own day, our own
lives, and the life of all Israel, and let us say Amen.
Let God's great name be blessed for ever and ever.
Let the name of God be glorified, exalted, and honored,
though God is beyond all the praises, songs, and adorations
that we can utter, and let us say Amen.
For us and for all Israel, may the blessing of peace and
the promise of life to come true, and let us say Amen.

May God who causes peace to reign in the high heavens,
let peace descend on us, on all Israel and all the world,
and let us say Amen.

GLOSSARY

Chasidei umot ha'olam. Righteous non-Jews.
Shoah. Holocaust; literally, "conflagration by fire."
Reishit tz'michat g'ulateinu. "The beginning of the flowering
   of our redemption."
Yahrzeit. Yearly anniversary marking the date of one's death.

Shavuot

Shavuot

"Entreat me not to leave you, for wherever you go I will go, wherever you lodge I will lodge, your people will be my people and your God will be my God" (Ruth 1:16). With these beautiful and simple words, read during the festival of Shavuot, Ruth the Moabite chose to become an Israelite and embrace the one God. Every year, in the late spring, the Jewish people celebrate the giving of the Torah (symbolizing God's covenant with the Israelites) with the festival of Shavuot. At Sinai, God and the children of Israel entered into an eternal covenant. The Jewish people promised to observe God's instructions and keep them as a priceless heritage. Celebrating Shavuot is our opportunity to again reenact and renew that ancient covenant with God.

BACK TO BASICS

Shavuot is the only holiday to which we keep looking forward by counting the days until it arrives. This we do when we count the *Omer* from Passover on, thus heightening our anticipation of the day. Shavuot is the shortest of the three biblical pilgrimage festivals. Although it lasts only two days, it continues to remain high in intensity of feeling since it reenacts the Revelation of God at Mount Sinai and the giving of the Torah.

Shavuot began as a spring harvest festival in Israel. The first wheat ripened approximately fifty days after the first barley. The first barley offering was brought to the Temple one day after Passover began. From that day on, the Jewish people were told to count seven complete weeks from one harvest to the other, and at the end of the counting they were commanded to celebrate the festival of Shavuot, which literally means "weeks." The Torah also refers to Shavuot as *Chag Habikkurim*, the Festival of the First Fruits. Jews would make their pilgrimage to Jerusalem bearing gift offerings of first fruits.

With the passing of time, Shavuot became more a celebration of God's revelation and less a celebration of the harvest.

CALENDAR

Shavuot falls on the sixth and seventh day of Sivan, and is celebrated for two days. In Israel and in Reform Judaism it is celebrated for one day. In contrast to Passover and Sukkot, which celebrate a physical redemption, most of the preparations for Shavuot concern the spirit and require no physical objects.

For some people, the most important preparation for Shavuot is a lengthy nap on the eve of Shavuot. This is because many communities sponsor a *tikkun leil shavuot*, an all night study session. Originating with the mystics, there is a passage in the mystical work called the *Zohar* that praises those who stay awake all night in anticipation of receiving the Torah.

In some European Jewish communities it was the custom to begin teaching children Torah on Shavuot. As the letters of the Hebrew alphabet were being taught and mastered, the teacher would give the students some honey symbolizing the sweetness of Jewish education. Today in religious schools students are often presented with their own book of the Bible on Shavuot. Many Hebrew High schools hold their confirmation exercises at one of the Shavuot services. At these services which are often led by the students, diplomas are presented along with certificates of confirmation. Bringing people into the covenant of God and having them symbolically strengthen their commitment to Judaism and affirm their faith is what Shavuot is really all about.

CELEBRATIONS

In the Synagogue

Many synagogues are often decorated with flowers, leaves and plants on Shavuot. Perhaps this is a reminder of Mount Sinai which was green with plants and shrubs, or it may be a symbol of the harvest which was brought to the Temple.The evening of the first night of Shavuot is often used for synagogues that have a Hebrew High School confirmation class. Students in such a class will often lead services as well as put on an original cantata with a theme link to Shavuot. Following this service is the study session using a special booklet called a *Tikkun*, which contains portions from all thirty nine books of the Bible, as well as other sacred writings. Many pious Jews sit up throughout the night studying the *Tikkun*, demonstrating their deep love for the study of the Torah.

During the synagogue services of the first day there are three very special highlights. First, the Torah reading on the first day is the Revelation of the Ten Commandments (Exodus 19:1-20:26.). Our rabbis tell us that in every generation each of us should consider him/herself as having personally received the Torah on Mount Sinai. As we reach the section of the Ten Commandments, the entire congregation stands for its reading, adding to the excitement!

The second feature of the morning is the reading of *Akdamut*, eleventh century liturgical poems of loyalty of Jews to the Torah and God's love for Israel.

The last feature of the morning is the reading of the Book of Ruth, or selections from it. The book tells the story of Ruth, a young Moabite woman who chose to convert to Judaism. One of her later descendants was King David, who died on Shavuot and from whose line tradition says the Messiah will come. Appropriately, the story of Ruth takes place during harvest time.

On the second day of the Shavuot holiday, as on the final day of all festivals, the *Yizkor* memorial prayer is recited. The reading of the Torah for that day includes a detailed description of the Biblical celebration of the Three Pilgrimmage Festivals and the duty to appear before God and bring free-will offerings.

The Sephardic Jews developed a beautiful ritual for Shavuot. Immediately after opening the ark on Shavuot morning, Sephardic Jews read a *ketubah*, a marriage contract between God (the groom) and Israel (the bride). In the *ketubah* God invites the bride to the palace and promises to bind to her forever. The bride says "We will do and we will listen," the exact words that were used by the Israelites at Mount Sinai.

In the Home
All of the festival rules regarding candlelighting, *Kiddush* over wine, blessings over washing hands, bread and after the meal apply to Shavuot. But there are some exceptions, which give the holiday its own special character.

On Shavuot, it is customary to eat dairy foods and not meat as in other Jewish festivals. Foods like cheese *blintzes*, *kreplach* and cheesecake are served. Jewish lore offers several origins to the dairy tradition. One explanation grew out of the allusion to the verse in the Song of Songs (4:11) that the "knowledge of the Torah is like milk and honey under the tongue." Another reason is that until the Jews received the Torah they were not bound by the Jewish dietary laws of *kashrut*. Upon receiving the Torah all of their pans and pots were rendered unkosher so they ate dairy until they became more familiar with the kosher laws.

Another food custom is to prepare or buy *challot* that are longer than usual, symbolic of the "wave offering". These were the bread loaves that the Jews were required to bring to the Temple on Shavuot.

In addition to food customs, a tradition arose to decorate the home with plants, flowers and tree branches, symbolic of the spring harvest.

BASIC BLESSINGS

Candlelighting

בָּרוּךְ אַתָּה יהוה אֱלֹהֵינוּ מֶלֶךְ הָעוֹלָם, אֲשֶׁר קִדְּשָׁנוּ בְּמִצְוֹתָיו וְצִוָּנוּ לְהַדְלִיק נֵר שֶׁל (שַׁבָּת וְשֶׁל) יוֹם טוֹב.

Barukh atah adonai eloheinu melekh ha'olam asher kid'shanu b'mitzvotav v'tzivanu l'hadlik neir shel (shabbat v'shel) yom tov.

Praised are You, Adonai our God, Sovereign of the Universe, who has made us holy by mitzvot and instructed us to kindle the (Shabbat and) festival candles.

Festival Kiddush over Wine

בָּרוּךְ אַתָּה יהוה אֱלֹהֵינוּ מֶלֶךְ הָעוֹלָם, בּוֹרֵא פְּרִי הַגָּפֶן
בָּרוּךְ אַתָּה יהוה אֱלֹהֵינוּ מֶלֶךְ הָעוֹלָם, אֲשֶׁר בָּחַר בָּנוּ מִכָּל־עָם
וְרוֹמְמָנוּ מִכָּל־לָשׁוֹן, וְקִדְּשָׁנוּ בְּמִצְוֹתָיו. וַתִּתֶּן לָנוּ יהוה אֱלֹהֵינוּ
בְּאַהֲבָה (שַׁבָּתוֹת לִמְנוּחָה וּ)מוֹעֲדִים לְשִׂמְחָה, חַגִּים וּזְמַנִּים לְשָׂשׂוֹן,
אֶת־יוֹם (הַשַּׁבָּת הַזֶּה וְאֶת־יוֹם) חַג הַשָּׁבוּעוֹת הַזֶּה, זְמַן מַתַּן תּוֹרָתֵנוּ,
(בְּאַהֲבָה) מִקְרָא קֹדֶשׁ, זֵכֶר לִיצִיאַת מִצְרָיִם. כִּי־בָנוּ בָחַרְתָּ וְאוֹתָנוּ
קִדַּשְׁתָּ מִכָּל־הָעַמִּים, (וְשַׁבָּת) וּמוֹעֲדֵי קָדְשֶׁךָ (בְּאַהֲבָה וּבְרָצוֹן)

בְּשִׂמְחָה וּבְשָׂשׂוֹן הִנְחַלְתָּנוּ. בָּרוּךְ אַתָּה יְיָ, מְקַדֵּשׁ (הַשַּׁבָּת וְ)
יִשְׂרָאֵל וְהַזְּמַנִּים.

*Barukh atah adonai eloheinu melekh ha'olam, borei p'ri
hagafen. Barukh atah adonai eloheinu melekh ha'olam,
asher bachar banu mikol am v'rom'manu mikol lashon
v'kid'shanu b'mitzvotav vatiten lanu adonai eloheinu b'ahavah (shabbatot lim'nuchah u) mo'adim l'simchah chagim
uzmanim l'sasson et yom (hashabbat hazeh v'et yom) chag
hashavuot hazeh, z'man matan torateinu (b'ahavah) mikra
kodesh zeikher litzi'at mitzrayim. Ki vanu vacharta v'otanu
kidashta mikol ha'amim (v'shabbat) umo'adei kodsh'kha
(b'ahavah uv'ratzon) b'simchah uv'sasson hinchaltanu.
Barukh atah adonai, m'kadesh (hashabbat v') yisra'eil
v'haz'manim.*

Praised are You, Eternal our God, Sovereign of the Universe
who creates fruit of the vine.
Praised are You, Eternal our God, Sovereign of the Universe
who has chosen and distinguished us from among all
others by adding holiness to our lives with mitzvot. Lovingly
have You given us (Shabbat for rest,) festivals for joy and
holidays for happiness, among them this (Shabbat and
this) day of Shavuot, season of the giving of the Torah, a
day of sacred assembly recalling the Exodus from Egypt.
Thus You have chosen us, endowing us with holiness
from among all peoples by granting us (Shabbat and)
Your hallowed festivals (lovingly and gladly) in happiness
and joy. Praised are You, God who hallows (Shabbat
and) the people Israel and the festivals.

Shehecheyanu

בָּרוּךְ אַתָּה יהוה אֱלֹהֵינוּ מֶלֶךְ הָעוֹלָם, שֶׁהֶחֱיָנוּ וְקִיְּמָנוּ וְהִגִּיעָנוּ
לַזְּמַן הַזֶּה.

*Barukh atah adonai eloheinu melekh ha'olam sheheche-
yanu v'kiymanu v'higi'anu laz'man hazeh.*

Praised are You, Adonai our God, Sovereign of the
Universe, who has kept us alive, sustained us, and helped
us to reach this moment.

N'tilat Yadayim (Washing the Hands)
*Grasp a cup or pitcher of water in your left hand and pour
some over the right. Reverse the process and repeat once or
twice. Recite this blessing:*

בָּרוּךְ אַתָּה יהוה אֱלֹהֵינוּ מֶלֶךְ הָעוֹלָם, אֲשֶׁר קִדְּשָׁנוּ בְּמִצְוֹתָיו
וְצִוָּנוּ עַל נְטִילַת יָדָיִם.

*Barukh atah adonai eloheinu melekh ha'olam asher
kid'shanu b'mitzvotav v'tzivanu al n'tilat yadayim.*

Praised are You, Adonai, Sovereign of the Universe, who
has made us holy by mitzvot and instructed us to wash
our hands.

Hamotzi

בָּרוּךְ אַתָּה יהוה אֱלֹהֵינוּ מֶלֶךְ הָעוֹלָם, הַמּוֹצִיא לֶחֶם מִן הָאָרֶץ.

*Barukh atah adonai eloheinu melekh ha'olam hamotzi
lechem min ha'aretz.*

Praised are You, Adonai our God, Sovereign of the Universe, who brings forth bread from the earth.

Blessing after Meal

רַבּוֹתַי נְבָרֵךְ.

Rabotai n'vareikh

Friends, let us give thanks.

The others respond, and the leader repeats:

יְהִי שֵׁם יְיָ מְבֹרָךְ מֵעַתָּה וְעַד עוֹלָם.

Y'hi sheim adonai m'vorakh mei'atah v'ad olam.

May God be praised now and forever.

The leader continues:

בִּרְשׁוּת רַבּוֹתַי, נְבָרֵךְ (אֱלֹהֵינוּ) שֶׁאָכַלְנוּ מִשֶּׁלּוֹ.

Bir'shut rabotai n'vareikh (eloheinu) she'akhalnu mishelo.

With your consent friends, let us praise (our God) the One of whose food we have partaken.

The others respond, and the leader repeats:

בָּרוּךְ (אֱלֹהֵינוּ) שֶׁאָכַלְנוּ מִשֶּׁלּוֹ וּבְטוּבוֹ חָיִינוּ.

Barukh (eloheinu) she'akhalnu mishelo uv'tuvo chayinu.

Praised be (our God) the One whose food we have partaken and by whose goodness we live.

Leader and others:

בָּרוּךְ הוּא וּבָרוּךְ שְׁמוֹ.

Barukh hu uvarukh sh'mo.

Praised be God and praised be God's name.

בָּרוּךְ אַתָּה יהוה אֱלֹהֵינוּ מֶלֶךְ הָעוֹלָם,הַזָּן אֶת־הָעוֹלָם כֻּלוֹ בְּטוּבוֹ, בְּחֵן בְּחֶסֶד וּבְרַחֲמִים. הוּא נוֹתֵן לֶחֶם לְכָל־בָּשָׂר כִּי לְעוֹלָם חַסְדּוֹ. וּבְטוּבוֹ הַגָּדוֹל תָּמִיד לֹא חָסַר לָנוּ וְאַל יֶחְסַר לָנוּ מָזוֹן לְעוֹלָם וָעֶד בַּעֲבוּר שְׁמוֹ הַגָּדוֹל, כִּי הוּא אֵל זָן וּמְפַרְנֵס לַכֹּל וּמֵטִיב לַכֹּל וּמֵכִין מָזוֹן לְכָל־בְּרִיּוֹתָיו אֲשֶׁר בָּרָא. בָּרוּךְ אַתָּה יהוה, הַזָּן אֶת־הַכֹּל.

Barukh atah adonai, eloheinu melekh ha'olam, hazan et ha'olam kulo b'tuvo b'chein, b'chesed, uv'rachamim. Hu notein lechem l'khol basar, ki l'olam chasdo. Uv'tuvo hagadol, tamid lo chasar lanu, v'al yechsar lanu mazon l'olam va'ed ba'avur sh'mo hagadol, ki hu el zan um'farneis lakol, umeitiv lakol, umeikhin mazon l'khol b'riyotav asher bara. Barukh atah adonai, hazan et hakol.

Praised are You, Eternal, our God, Sovereign of the Universe who sustains the whole world with kindness and compassion. You provide food for every creature, for Your love endures forever. Your great goodness has never failed us. Your great glory assures us nourishment. All life is God's creation and God is good to all, providing every creature with food and sustenance. Praised are You, God who sustains all life.

נוֹדֶה לְךָ יְיָ אֱלֹהֵינוּ עַל שֶׁהִנְחַלְתָּ לַאֲבוֹתֵינוּ אֶרֶץ חֶמְדָּה טוֹבָה
וּרְחָבָה, בְּרִית וְתוֹרָה, חַיִּים וּמָזוֹן. יִתְבָּרַךְ שִׁמְךָ בְּפִי כָל־חַי תָּמִיד
לְעוֹלָם וָעֶד, כַּכָּתוּב: וְאָכַלְתָּ וְשָׂבָעְתָּ וּבֵרַכְתָּ אֶת־יְיָ אֱלֹהֶיךָ עַל
הָאָרֶץ הַטּוֹבָה אֲשֶׁר נָתַן לָךְ. בָּרוּךְ אַתָּה יְיָ, עַל הָאָרֶץ וְעַל
הַמָּזוֹן.

Nodeh l'kha adonai eloheinu al shehinchalta la'avoteinu eretz chemdah, tovah ur'chavah, b'rit v'torah, chayim um-azon. Yitbarakh shimkha b'fi khol chai tamid l'olam va'ed. Kakatuv v'akhalta v'savata uveirakhta et adonai elohekha al ha'aretz hatovah asher natan lakh. Barukh atah adonai, al ha'aretz v'al hamazon.

We thank you, God, for the pleasing, ample, desirable land which You gave to our ancestors, for the covenant and Torah, for life and sustenance. May You forever be praised by all who live, as it is written in the Torah: "When you have eaten and are satisfied, you shall praise the Eternal your God for the good land which God has given you." Praised are You, God, for the land and for sustenance.

וּבְנֵה יְרוּשָׁלַיִם עִיר הַקֹּדֶשׁ בִּמְהֵרָה בְיָמֵינוּ. בָּרוּךְ אַתָּה יְיָ, בּוֹנֶה
בְרַחֲמָיו יְרוּשָׁלַיִם. אָמֵן.

Uv'neih yerushalayim ir hakodesh bimheirah v'yameinu. Barukh atah adonai, boneh v'rachamav yerushalayim. Amen.

Fully rebuild Jerusalem, the holy city, soon in our time. Praised are You, Adonai, who in mercy rebuilds Jerusalem. Amen.

בָּרוּךְ אַתָּה יהוה אֱלֹהֵינוּ מֶלֶךְ הָעוֹלָם, הַמֶּלֶךְ הַטּוֹב וְהַמֵּטִיב לַכֹּל. הוּא הֵטִיב, הוּא מֵטִיב, הוּא יֵיטִיב לָנוּ. הוּא גְמָלָנוּ הוּא גוֹמְלֵנוּ הוּא יִגְמְלֵנוּ לָעַד חֵן וָחֶסֶד וְרַחֲמִים וִיזַכֵּנוּ לִימוֹת הַמָּשִׁיחַ.

Barukh atah adonai, eloheinu melekh ha'olam, hamelekh hatov v'hameitiv lakol. Hu heitiv, hu meitiv, hu yeitiv lanu. Hu g'malanu, hu gomleinu, hu yigm'leinu la'ad chein vachesed v'rachamim, vizakeinu limot hamashi'ach.

Praised are You, God, Sovereign of the Universe who is good to all, whose goodness is constant through all time. Favor us with kindness and compassion now and in the future as in the past. May we be worthy of the days of the Messiah.

הָרַחֲמָן, הוּא יַנְחִילֵנוּ יוֹם שֶׁכֻּלּוֹ שַׁבָּת וּמְנוּחָה לְחַיֵּי הָעוֹלָמִים.

Harachaman hu yanchileinu yom shekulo shabbat umenu-chah l'chayei ha'olamim.

May the Merciful grant us a day of true shabbat rest, reflecting the life of eternity.

[On festivals:

הָרַחֲמָן, הוּא יַנְחִילֵנוּ יוֹם שֶׁכֻּלּוֹ טוֹב

Harachaman hu yanchileinu yom shekulo tov.

May the Merciful grant us a day filled with the spirit of the festival.]

וְנִשָּׂא בְרָכָה מֵאֵת יְיָ וּצְדָקָה מֵאֱלֹהֵי יִשְׁעֵנוּ וְנִמְצָא חֵן וְשֵׂכֶל טוֹב בְּעֵינֵי אֱלֹהִים וְאָדָם. עֹשֶׂה שָׁלוֹם בִּמְרוֹמָיו הוּא יַעֲשֶׂה שָׁלוֹם עָלֵינוּ וְעַל כָּל־יִשְׂרָאֵל, וְאִמְרוּ אָמֵן.

V'nisa v'rakhah mei'eit adonai utz'dakah mei'elohei yish'einu. V'nimtza chein v'seikhel tov b'einei elohim v'adam. Oseh shalom bimromav hu ya'aseh shalom aleinu v'al kol yisra'eil. V'imru amen.

May we receive blessings from God, loving-kindness from the God of our deliverance. May we find grace and good favor before God and all people. May God who brings peace to the universe bring peace to us and to all the people Israel. And let us say: Amen.

MAKING FAMILY

There are many family-oriented activities that you may wish to try with your own family on Shavuot. Here are several for you to try:

1. Discuss the Ten Commandments with your family (see Exodus chapter 20). Think of some other commandments that you would have like to have seen included among the original ten.

2. Make floral decorations for your Shavuot dinner table.

3. Read and discuss the Book of Ruth as a family.

4. Play Shavuot games with your family. Here is a brief description of the Shavuot game called *Jerusalem Pilgrimage*:

Purpose
To recall the ancient Biblical pilgrimage to Jerusalem on Shavuot.

Instructions

a. The first player begins by saying: "I am making a pilgrimage to Jerusalem. The first fruits I am bringing are figs."

b. The second player must repeat what the first one said and add another fruit or vegetable. For example, "I am making a pilgrimage to Jerusalem. The first fruits I am bringing are figs and oranges."

c. Each player in turn must repeat the preceding sentence, adding another fruit or vegetable.

d. If a player omits any fruit or vegetable, or does not recite them in the original sequence, or fails to add a new item, that player is eliminated from the game.

e. The last player to remain the the game wins.

5. Make a Mount Sinai cake and put the Ten Commandments on it.

6. Make some first fruit baskets and donate them to a food shelter.

GLOSSARY

Akdamut. A special poem read on Shavuot.

Bikkurim. First fruits.

Chag Habikkurim. Festival of First Fruits, another name for Shavuot.

Chag Hakatzir. Festival of the Harvest, another name for Shavuot.

Omer. The measure of grain which was to be brought into the Temple during the seven weeks from Passover to Shavuot.

Ruth. The Moabite woman who accepted the Jewish religion.
    She was the great grandmother of King David.
Sivan. The Hebrew month in which Shavuot falls.
Tikkun. The special booklet read the first night of Shavuot,
    containing portions of every Bible book and other holy
    writings.

Tisha B'av

Tisha B'av

"By the rivers of Babylon we sat and cried when we remembered Zion" (Psalm 137). Undoubtedly the darkest day in the Jewish calendar is Tisha B'av, the ninth of Av. Not only have many great disasters befallen the Jewish people on this date, but all the subsequent calamities have been a direct consequence of the destruction of the two Temples, which took place on this day, and of our exile from Israel, which followed the mass destruction. On Tisha B'av we remember the past and apply its lesson to the present. We are exhorted never to lose faith in God at times of great calamity, but to pray and strive for a brighter future. And the message of the Midrash is a spectacular one of hope: "The Messiah was born on the day that the Temple was destroyed." Our sages yearned for the time when Tisha B'av, along with all the other fast-days, would be turned into a day of gladness and rejoicing.

BACK TO BASICS

The ninth of Av is a universal day of Jewish mourning. On it Jews mourn many historical events, including the destruction of the two Jerusalem Temples and the expulsion from Spain in 1492. The prophet Jeremiah, who witnessed the destruction of the First Temple, left in the Book of Lamentations (known in Hebrew as Eicha) his vivid impressions of the disaster. This book is chanted in a mournful and sad way, with worshippers in some synagogues sitting on low benches or on the floor as a sign of mourning.

Some people observe the nine days before Tisha B'av as a mourning period. During that time they do not get haircuts, go swimming, or eat meat, a symbol of luxury. During the actual fast on Tisha B'av, the same restrictions that apply to Yom Kippur apply: no eating or drinking, no anointing (i.e., cosmetics), no wearing leather shoes, and no sexual relations. In addition, the rabbis also prohibited the study of Torah (except for the Book of Job and certain prophetic books related directly to the Temple destruction). The reason for this was that "the study of Torah gladdens the soul," and Tisha B'av is not a day for being glad.

CALENDAR

Three weeks before Tisha B'av, on the seventeenth of Tammuz, the mourning cycle officially begins with the minor fast of Shiva Asar B'tammuz. On this day the walls around Jerusalem were penetrated by the enemy. Between Shiva Asar B'tammuz and Tisha B'av is a span of three weeks. During the so-called Three Weeks, many people do not celebrate weddings or play joyful music.

The latter part of the Three Weeks, from the first to the ninth of Av, is known as the Nine Days. During these days the laws of mourning intensify, with restrictions that often include a ban on swimming and eating meat. Likewise there is no drinking of wine, except for Shabbat.

OBSERVANCES

In the Synagogue

The synagogue services on Tisha B'av are most unusual. The room where the evening service is held often has its lights dimmed, and candles are lit. The prayers are spoken rather than chanted with melody. The reading of the Book of Lamentations is chanted using special musical notations that create a tone of weeping and mourning. Knowledgeable congregants often take turns reading different sections of the book. During the service there may be a discussion related to the themes of tragedy and destruction, often led by the rabbi.

The morning service the next day is also unique. The tallit (prayer shawl) and tefillin (phylacteries) are not worn, as a sign of mourning. Special prayers of mourning, called kinot are read during this service. There is a reading from the Torah (Deuteronomy 4:25–40) whose theme is the punishment of Israel for its sins, and opportunity and hope for redemption. In the Haftarah of the morning (which is chanted in the same mournful melody as Eicha) Jeremiah speaks of the despair of the Israelites, describing Jerusalem as a total wasteland.

During the afternoon Mincha service the mood of Tisha B'av becomes more hopeful. Tallit and tefillin are worn at this service. Both the Torah reading and the Haftarah of this service are the same as on all other public fasts, describing the Thirteen Attributes of God and the promise of salvation. Special prayers of comfort (Nachemta) are also a feature of this service.

The evening service marks the official end of the fast of Tisha B'av.

In the Home

Because Tisha B'av is a fast-day, it is subject to the same limitations as Yom Kippur. Basic traditional home observances include abstention not only from food but also from bathing, anointing oneself with cosmetics, wearing leather shoes, and sexual relations. In addition, books such as Job and other works that speak of sad events are read and even studied on this day. If Tisha B'av falls on a Sabbath it is postponed until Sunday, since on the Sabbath one may neither fast nor mourn publicly.

BASIC BLESSINGS

During the Mincha Amidah

בָּרוּךְ אַתָּה יהוה מְנַחֵם צִיּוֹן וּבוֹנֶה יְרוּשָׁלָיִם

Barukh atah adonai m'nacheim tziyon uvoneih yerushalayim.

Praised are You, Adonai, who comforts Zion and rebuilds Jerusalem.

GLOSSARY

Av. Month in which Tisha B'av falls.
Book of Lamentations. Biblical book read on the night of Tisha B'av, describing the destruction of Jerusalem.
Eicha. Hebrew name for Book of Lamentations.
Kinot. Special prayers of mourning and deep sadness read on Tisha B'av.

Nine Days. Days between the first and the ninth of Av when
   mourning customs are heightened.
Ninth of Av. English name for Tisha B'av.
Seventeenth of Tammuz. Fast commemorating the first breach
   in the walls of Jerusalem, which led to its destruction.
Three Weeks. Days of mourning between the seventeenth of
   Tammuz and the ninth of Av.

Holiday Connections for Making Family

1. Save New Year's cards and hang them up in the sukkah.

2. Make marmalade from the etrog at Sukkot and serve it at Hanukkah with latkes, or sweeten it and use it as a filling for sufganiyot.

3. Plant the seeds from your etrog and distribute them (as plants) during Tu Bishevat.

4. Use the lulav from Sukkot for *b'dikat chametz*, sweeping the corners of the room, or to ignite the fire when you burn the chametz at Pesach.

5. On Tu Bishevat, plant parsley indoors to be harvested and used for Pesach.

6. In order to relate Pesach to Shavuot, for those who count the omer, save one canned food each day between Pesach and Shavuot, to be given to a local food collective at Shavuot.

7. After your Tu Bishevat Seder, make preserves from your fruits to be used for filling hamantaschen at Purim.

8. Using liquid embroidery paints on a giant white tablecloth, encourage families to draw something or sign their names with notes for each holiday—so that the tablecloth begins empty at Rosh Hashanah and is filled by the following New Year.

9. Take your left-over Hanukkah candles and melt them into a giant Havdalah candle to be used each week during the year. Don't forget to add two or three new long wicks.

For Further Reading

Bloch, Abraham. *Biblical and Historical Background of Jewish Holy Days*. New York, 1980.

Cardozo, Arlene Rossen. *Jewish Family Celebrations*. New York, 1982.

Epstein, Morris. *All About Jewish Holidays and Customs*. New York, 1959.

Gaster, Theodor H. *Festivals of the Jewish Year*. New York, 1952.

Greenberg, Blu. *How to Run a Jewish Household*. New York, 1983.

Knobel, Peter S. *Gates of the Seasons*. New York, 1983.

Olitzky, Kerry M. and Ronald H. Isaacs. *The How-to Handbook of Jewish Living*. Hoboken, NJ, 1993.

Schauss, Hayyim. *Guide to the Jewish Holy Days*. New York, 1938.

Strassfeld, Michael. *The Jewish Holidays: A Guide and Commentary*. New York, 1985.

Trepp, Leo. *The Complete Book of Jewish Observance*. New York, 1980.

Waskow, Arthur. *Seasons of Our Joy*. New York, 1982.